ADVICE FROM DANIEL FOR ADDRESSING TODAY'S CULTURE

O. S. HAWKINS

ISBN: 0-9671584-5-1
Dewey Decimal Classification: 224.5 dc21
Subject Heading: BIBLE.O.T.DANIEL
Printed in the United States of America

Other books by O.S. Hawkins

When Revival Comes

After Revival Comes

Clues to a Successful Life

Where Angels Fear to Tread

Tracing the Rainbow Through the Rain

Unmasked: Recognizing and Dealing with Imposters in the Church

Revive Us Again

Jonah: Meeting the God of the Second Chance

Getting Down to Brass Tacks: Advice from James for Real World Christians

In Sheep's Clothing

Tearing Down Walls and Building Bridges

Moral Earthquakes and Secret Faults

Rebuilding: It's Never too Late for a New Beginning

Money Talks: But What Is It Really Saying?

Shields of Brass or Shields of Gold? Re-establishing a Standard of Excellence in the Church of the Lord Jesus Christ

Good News for Great Days

Drawing the Net

Dedication

To Reverend Ed and Ramona Enriquez

Together they faithfully served Southern Baptist churches and ministered to migrant workers over a lifetime of ministry. They represent the thousands of our dear retired pastors and, in many cases, their widows who are a part of our Adopt An Annuitant ministry. It is our privilege to "rise up before the gray headed and honor the presence" of these aged soldiers of the cross. The Annuity Board is committed to continue raising the necessary supplemental funds to meet their needs in their declining years...lest we forget!

Table of contents

A personal note from O.S. Hawkins

If you serve in a Southern Baptist church these paragraphs are unapologetically for you and they could be some of the most important paragraphs you will read. Although you will never "retire" from ministry there will come a day when you will retire from vocational church service. We want that to be a great day for you. And it can be, if you are prepared.

It is important to get started early in retirement planning. There is a thing called compound interest, which is extremely powerful. Let me illustrate. For example, assuming an 8% annual return, if a 25-year-old minister put $50 per month in his retirement account it would be worth $174,550 at age 65. If the same person waited until just the age of 35 to begin saving for retirement with the same $50 per month it would be worth $74,520 at age 65, a difference of $100,000. It is very important to start early, but it is also important to start wherever you are along the way to retirement.

The beautiful and beneficial part of being in the Annuity Board's Church Annuity Plan is the protection section. Did you know that if you or your church contributes only a few dollars per month to your retirement you automatically receive at no cost a survivor's benefit worth up to $100,000 to whomever you designate as your beneficiary? You also receive at no cost a $500 per month disability benefit simply by being a part of the Annuity Board retirement program. This benefit is a cooperative effort provided by your state Baptist convention and the Annuity Board and is a safety net every church should utilize for their ministers.

We at the Annuity Board want to be a Life Partner™ with you throughout your entire ministry. This is the driving reason behind our new products which now give you additional opportunities to save for retirement, or whatever your saving needs. You now have available to you savings vehicles in addition to your regular 403(b) plan that include Personal Investing Accounts and IRAs (Traditional and Roth IRAs). These opportunities are also available to spouses of persons eligible to participate in Annuity Board plans. Perhaps you have a retirement accumulation in a 401(k) plan from a previous employer. You may want to consider "rolling over" that accumulation into your retirement account or into a rollover IRA.

For more information about these new personal investing products, matching contributions from your state conventions, the protection section at no cost, housing allowance advantages in retirement, our mission church assistance fund, our relief ministries or any of our other services visit us on the world wide web at *www.absbc.org* or better yet call us at **1-800-262-0511** and speak personally to one of our customer relations specialists.

O.S. Hawkins

Introduction

Our current contemporary culture brings new challenges to our Christian faith with each passing day. Daniel was a young man who grew up in a Judeo culture of traditional family values. Then he unexpectedly found himself in a culture that was foreign to everything he had known. His value system, his truth claims, his moral compass was challenged repeatedly at every turn. His world evolved into a world of pluralism and paganism. Daniel could have blamed his challenging circumstances on societal ills, the court system of his day, the government, the media, the educational system or any number of a myriad of other places where Christians in our contemporary culture point fingers of accusation today. However, Daniel seems to step out of the Scripture and into our modern culture to show us some principles that will enable us not only to exist in our culture, but also to engage it and even thrive in it as well.

Like Daniel, we too find ourselves in a world that has passed from a Judeo-Christian culture to one which in many ways has become an anti-Judeo-Christian one. He has left us a book in the Old Testament that bears his name which is filled with contemporary applications that enable us to put into practice some time-honored biblical principles for addressing our contemporary world.

Can we really expect to change a crumbling culture around us? It is interesting to watch the church of Jesus Christ in the various ways it attempts to address the culture today. Some *compromise*—that is, they allow the permeating, pluralistic philosophy of the day to subtly take away the focus from the exclusivity of Christ. Others *condone* the culture. For some it is much easier to adapt to the culture and condone alternative lifestyles, not only in the pew but also in the pulpit. There are others who *condemn*. Some people respond to the culture by simply beating their Bibles a little harder and screaming a little louder as though that were going to win a lost generation. And thank God there are some who learn from Daniel to *confront* the culture and engage it by speaking the truth in love.

Francis Schaeffer was a 20th century cultural prophet. Several decades ago he predicted that we in the Western world would pass from a Judeo-Christian culture to a post-Judeo-Christian culture. Dr. Schaeffer lived to see his prophecy come true. If he were alive today he would look around our world and rightly exclaim that now we have moved to an anti-Judeo-Christian culture. Look around us. A few years ago one's failures and perversions were occasions of shame, guilt or embarrassment. This is not true in our modern culture. For some today those same things are occasions to star on television talk shows. The culture that permeates our society in America today is chronically sick and without moorings.

We have evolved into a schizophrenic society. Think about it. We listen to Billy Graham pray at presidential inaugurals and then punish schoolchildren who try to pray at graduations or football games. We watch our president and other elected leaders put their hands on the Bible to take the oath of office, but school administrators are fired for opening the same Bible to give counsel to wayward students. We cry out for law and order in our streets and at the same time some teach in the classroom that there are no moral absolutes. We cry out to stop so many illegitimate births and allow the government to subsidize the type of behavior that guarantees its rise. We're concerned about the high rate of teens involved in sex and instead of emphasizing abstinence, many of our administrators give them condoms in the schools. We say we have a dire need for the family to stay together and at the same time we liberalize divorce laws so that it becomes easier and easier simply to walk away. This is the culture we are called to engage and reach. This is the post-modern world around us. So many Christians hunker down behind the stained glass walls of their churches and shelter themselves from the world. They manifest an isolationism instead of an insulationism. Therefore, some of us live and think like we still are in a world that is governed by an ethic and a culture that is compatible and compassionate with the truth of the Bible. This is the only world some of us in the church know. And that would be all right if Christ had not given us a command to win our world to Himself. Unfortunately, the world around us does not share our values or our truth claims.

The early church in the Book of Acts exploded when Paul and others stepped out of their comfort zones and engaged a culture that was different from their own. Our 21st century world is more like the 1st century than perhaps any other century. We're called upon to engage a culture that is not interested in our formulas nor our stained glass windows nor our organs. We're called to engage a culture that is not asking if the Bible is true. It is asking if it is relevant. Our culture wants to know if the Book of our faith written in an ancient Middle-Eastern world has any relevancy in our world where we're transplanting organs, experimenting with genetic engineering, and sending people to the moon and back.

Many of us who are reading these words were brought up in a Judeo-Christian culture. I certainly was. I have vivid memories of prayers being heard on the public address system at D. McRae Elementary School in Fort Worth. I remember seeing the Ten Commandments on the wall of my classroom. I remember hearing daily Bible reading in the classroom. I remember the good and godly folks we called Gideons handing out New Testaments in our school. I remember when the church was the most respected and esteemed institution in the city. This is not the world we're called to reach today.

A lot of the problem in seeking to reach the lost generations in America today is rooted in the fact that so often the church cannot determine the difference between what is biblical and what is cultural. Therefore, we go on holding to our cultural wineskins that worked so well a generation ago when we were engaging a Judeo-Christian culture. They worked fairly well when we were still immersed in a post-Judeo-Christian culture, but today our wineskins are leaking profusely. Many churches are empty today because we hold on to cultural expressions that do not apply to a modern culture.

The events of September 11, 2001, have left an indelible mark on the American psyche. Now is the church's moment to rise up and capture a culture. Daniel was a young man who suddenly found himself in a culture that was foreign to everything that he'd known as a youngster. He steps out of the pages of Scripture and into our world today with some valuable principles that give us tremendous advice in confronting our own culture. As we journey together through these pages let's listen carefully to him and learn from him how to not only exist in the cultural of our day but to engage it as well.

Part One

The remote control syndrome

My wife Susie and I have enjoyed over 30 years of marriage. We seldom have conflict but on a recent evening it was a different story. The object of our spat was that little black handheld gadget we call the television remote control. On that given evening we were lying in bed and she was trying to go to sleep. I was happily engaged with the remote control moving from one news station to another as I surfed the channels. All of a sudden she sat up in bed and "faster than a speeding bullet and more powerful than a locomotive" she reached over and grabbed it out of my hand! Guess what? I did not like that. Why? Just think about what that little gadget is called. The remote "control." We like to be in control of things around us. I did not like it when she had control of the TV. I found myself out of control. Holding the controls and circumstances of life gives us a sense of security. There's just something about us that likes to be in control.

Daniel is the story of a young man, like so many young men today, who suddenly finds himself in a situation in which he has no control. He was out of his comfort zone. He had been taken from everything he had known in his Judeo culture in Judah to the foreign pagan culture of Babylon. The remote control had been jerked from his hand.

When we hear the name Daniel some of us think of an out-of-date prophet. Some have the idea that he was some old guy with no idea of what it's like to live in a culture like ours with our struggles and challenges. Daniel was a real guy, living in a real world with real problems. He had a real job in the real marketplace. He was surrounded by real men and women in his office who were hostile to his belief system and to his faith. They had their own new age applications to life. In fact, in the fifth chapter of the book that bears his name we will find him at a real office party with alcohol and women everywhere. His bosses were real. They were vain and undercutting. They took credit for other people's work while trying to get ahead themselves.

Daniel would have felt right at home in our modern secular workplace. This is the Daniel who speaks to us from the pages of Scripture. He has a lot to say to us today. He provides a lot of do's and don'ts for not simply surviving in an anti-Christian culture but succeeding and truly engaging it to make a long-term difference.

This week the people in our pews will live out there in a pagan culture during the week. Tomorrow our young people will go to many schools where they will be confronted with value systems that are foreign to what they hear on Sundays. We all find ourselves living in a world with standards and principles that are foreign to the Bible. The truth is, preachers are not my real heroes. My heroes are businessmen and women who stand for Christ in the marketplace, out there in the culture where they can really make a difference.

The story of Daniel is the story of a man who understands our challenges. It is the story of someone who was confronted with the same difficulties and hard decisions that we are called upon to make every day. He was plopped down in a culture that pressured him to stuff his religious roots way back in the corner of the office closet. He found himself in a world that tempted him to take the easy way to the top. Yet, his is a story that offers help and hope. Daniel is an inspiration to all of us who face cultural clashes every day in our post-modern world.

God took Daniel out of a comfortable culture where he had been all of his life and placed him in a godless environment with a different language, a different literature, and a different lifestyle. There's a sense in which the same thing has happened in our world today. We no longer live in the midst of a culture that shares our convictions. We have lost the home court advantage. We, too, find ourselves living in a culture that's speaking a different language, reading a different literature, and living a different lifestyle. Let's face it, the Babylonian culture of the 21st century is the United States of America. Men and women in today's marketplace are faced with increasing cultural difficulties as they seek to succeed in business and maintain their integrity at the same time.

What shall we as followers of Jesus Christ do in the midst of this cultural shift? How are we going to stand? Let's invite Daniel to speak to us. He has been there. He has done that. He knows what it is to have the remote control taken from him, to have no control over what is going on around him. He lived in a culture that stood against everything he had been taught.

What advice does Daniel have for us today? He says three basic things to us. First, *"Don't give in...be resistant."* Our tendency is simply to give in to the culture and go its way. In fact, Daniel did give in on some things that were nonessentials but he drew the line on certain things. He made some tough decisions that were not compromised. Daniel did not isolate himself from the culture but he certainly insulated himself from it. He drew the line when the issue became contrary to scriptural principles.

Secondly, Daniel says to us *"Don't give up...be consistent."* Our tendency is to become so overwhelmed by a culture around us that we simply want to give up even trying to hold on to biblical principles in the marketplace. If Daniel is saying anything to us today it is this: don't give up, be consistent.

He also speaks to us across the centuries and says, *"Don't give out...be persistent."* I love the words we find in Daniel 1:21, *thus Daniel continued.* Daniel was in it for the long haul. He finished strongly. He was persistent. It took time but he won in the end and his influence made an incredible difference. The Book of Daniel is speaking to our modern world today. Daniel's words are not simply theoretical. They've been beaten out on the anvil of personal experience. He knows what we're up against. He has walked where we are walking. He's been there and left us a pattern to follow. He speaks to us today and says, "Don't give in, be resistant. Don't give up, be consistent. Don't give out, be persistent."

Chapter 1

Don't give in...be resistant

Dan. 1: 1-8

Daniel was keenly aware of the tendency to simply give in to the culture around us. Sadly, this is happening in so many churches today. Some of us with good intentions have leaned over looking into the culture and studying it so long we've actually fallen into it ourselves. I do not believe Daniel is speaking softly here in these opening verses of Chapter 1. He is passionate. He is saying, "Don't give in, be resistant." He draws the line. He does not draw the line on nonessentials. He draws the line when it comes to the Word of God. This is the point at which he resisted. He didn't give in to a culture around him. He made some tough decisions. In order to see a picture of the biblical background that brought him to this platform we must ask ourselves a few questions.

We should begin by asking the "where?" question. Where does Daniel take place? There are two places mentioned in the early verses of his book. One is Judah. After the reign of King Solomon the twelve tribes of Israel divided. There were ten tribes in the Northern Kingdom and two tribes in the Southern Kingdom. Judah and Benjamin were in the south. Jerusalem was the capital of the Southern Kingdom. They had 19 kings that ruled over them over a period of three and a half centuries. Eleven of those kings were bad and eight of them were relatively good. In contrast, the Northern Kingdom never had one good king. They went into the Assyrian captivity in 722 B.C. Thus, Judah is the Southern Kingdom. The Southern Kingdom is where Daniel was born and raised. The other place mentioned is Babylon. All humanistic thought can trace its journey back there to the Tower of Babel (Gen. 11). In Daniel's day the Babylonian Empire was the world power. Its capital was about 50 miles from the modern city of Baghdad, Iraq. Babylon was the capital of pagan worship and was without question the world power of its day.

Next we come to the "who?" question. Again, we're introduced to several people. There is Nebuchadnezzar, the King of Babylon. He designed the wonders of Babylon. Nebuchadnezzar was an amazing man who built an incredible city and developed a world empire. We also are introduced to Jehoiakim who was the king of the Southern Kingdom at the time. He was nothing more than a puppet. He led the Jews by inner-corruption to worship other gods and *did evil in the sight of the Lord.* (2 Kings 24:19) The Bible tells us that he filled Jerusalem *with innocent blood.* (2 Kings 24:4)

We're also introduced to a young man named Daniel who was a descendant of good King Hezikiah. He was a boy under the revival of Josiah and that move of God's Spirit had a profound impact upon his life. He was an extremely bright young man who, if he had lived today, would have been the type of young man who would have had an appointment to one of the military academies or one of the respected institutions of higher learning in our world. His world was turned upside down when he was taken into Babylonian captivity by Nebuchadnezzar with the first group of exiles in 605 B.C.

Next we come to the "when?" question. Daniel 1:1 tells us that these events took place in *the third year of the reign of Jehoiakim.* That is, 605 B.C. These were days of severe punishment for Judah. A group of bright and outstanding young future leaders were taken captive to Babylon. In 597 B.C. another group was exiled. Then, in 586 B.C. the Jewish temple in Jerusalem and the city of gold herself were laid waste and destroyed and the rest of the remnant was taken into Babylonian exile. Thus, by the time the captivity was complete Daniel had already been living in Babylon for almost 20 years.

This brings us to the "what?" question. What was this that was taking place? It was nothing short of the judgment of God. God was punishing His people. In fact, the Bible puts it like this; *the Lord gave Jehoiakim king of Judah into his* [Nebuchadnezzar] *hand.* (Dan. 1:2) God was in control. God was pushing the buttons on His own remote control.

There's a sense in which Nebuchadnezzar was nothing more than the remote control in the hand of God Himself. In fact, in Jeremiah 25:9 He refers to Nebuchadnezzar as *my servant*. Some of us in our modern day have forgotten that God judges sin. The Babylonian captivity was the direct judgment of God upon His people. This captivity into Babylon had been predicted in detail years before it happened (Isa. 39:5-7; Jer. 25:8-12; II Kings 20:17-18). However, Judah would not repent. Judah had seen what had happened to the Northern Kingdom. Judah had heard the warnings of Isaiah and Jeremiah and Hezekiah. Judah had been spared by miraculous intervention during the Assyrian invasion. They got to the place where they began to think they were indestructible. Can we help but think of our own America? Most of us today are not hearing God's warning to us, much less heeding it.

Thus, Judah was taken away into the captivity of a pagan world and culture. One only has to read Psalm 137 to see what it was like. *By the rivers of Babylon, there we sat down, yea, we wept when we remembered Zion. We hung our harps upon the willows in the midst of it. …How shall we sing the Lord's song in a foreign land?* (Psa. 137:1-6) Daniel reminds us that it is the hand of God that is in the rise and fall of nations (Dan. 2:21). Yes, the Lord gave Jehoiakim, King of Judah, into Nebuchadnezzar's hand. If God would do that with a people He called the "apple of His eye" what makes us think that we are so invincible here in America? The Babylonian captivity was nothing less than a judgment of God upon His own people.

Finally, we come to the "why?" question. Why did God allow it? God allowed the Babylonian captivity to scourge His people. The Bible says, *Whom the Lord loves He chastens.* (Heb. 12:6) God punishes His own people out of a heart of love for them. Not only was the captivity to scourge His people but to purge His people. There were many good things that came out of the Babylonian captivity. Israel never again followed after idols, not even until this day. The Old Testament began to come together under men like Ezra. The remnant returned to Jerusalem and in it was the seed of our Messiah. In captivity Daniel and the others carried the message of God to heathen lands. Centuries later when the Magi would come from the East to worship the Christ Child we would be reminded that they heard about Him because of the witness of a young man named Daniel that was handed down through the generations in their geographical vicinity.

There's an interesting plot that unfolds in Daniel 1:3-7. Nebuchadnezzar's plan was to gather the brightest young Jewish minds and bring them into the Babylonian environment and culture. He set out to re-educate them and to retrain them. His plot and plan was to eventually place them in charge of the coming exiles and then one day place them back in their home country to rule there on behalf of Babylon. It was a clever plot. These young men who accompanied Daniel into exile had impressive resumes (see Dan. 1:4). They were young men with no physical defects. They were handsome. They had high SAT scores. They were well informed. They were equipped to understand. They had social graces. Nebuchadnezzar's plan was to brainwash these monotheistic boys into polytheistic Babylonian leaders.

He set out to change their language (Dan. 1:4). To be accepted in any new culture one needs to learn the language. The first thing Nebuchadnezzar did was to change the language of Zion to the Babylonian language. Anyone on the mission field today knows the necessity of this. Southern Baptists are sending unprecedented numbers of missionaries around the world today. One of the first things they do before engaging their various new cultures is to learn the language of the people.

Nebuchadnezzar also set out to change their literature (Dan. 1:4). Literature is the window through which most cultures present themselves. The king sought to fill these young minds with Babylonian philosophy, Babylonian science, Babylonian astrology, and Babylonian religion. His goal was to re-educate them away from the roots of their previous belief system and all of its traditional values. We're doing that in America today and simply call it "values clarification" in many public education systems.

Nebuchadnezzar not only set out to change their language and literature but also their lifestyle (Dan. 1:5). He appointed daily provisions of his own delicacies. In other words, these boys were provided with gourmet delights straight from the King's table. Now remember these boys were Jews and lived by a strict kosher diet. Nebuchadnezzar's intent here was far more than simply introducing them to new food, he was about the business of seeking to change their very lifestyle.

Nebuchadnezzar also sought to change their loyalty (Dan. 1:7). He did this by changing their names. All four of these young men's names spoke about who they were and from whence they'd come. Daniel's name meant "God is my judge." Hananiah's name meant "beloved of the Lord." Mishael's name meant "who is like God." Azariah's name meant "the Lord is my help." These were the names of the young men who accompanied Daniel into Babylonian exile from Judah. All of their names were changed to Babylonian names, which were related not to Jehovah but to Babylonian deities. Nebuchadnezzar was seeking to change their loyalties. He wanted to train these young people to handle Jewish affairs of the exiles and then rule over the people once they were back home in Jerusalem. They had tremendous leadership abilities. His goal was clear. He set out to change their very way of thinking and their very loyalties.

We look at this today and say that is terrible. Yes, but we should look more closely around us. Our brightest young minds are being re-educated and retrained by humanistic philosophy right here in America. In 1933 the Humanist Manifesto set out its plain objectives and no one paid much attention. In 1973 the Humanist Manifesto II set out its goals. And what were the goals of this Humanist Manifesto? It set out to "bring young people to deny the deity of God and the biblical account of creation. It set out to re-educate young people to the fact that moral values should be self-determined and situational." That is, there should be no absolute truth. They set out to remove distinctions between the roles of male and females. They set out to advocate a sexual freedom between consenting individuals regardless of their age or preferences. They set out to advocate the right to abortion and euthanasia. And they also argued for the equal distribution of American wealth to reduce poverty. They were intent on controlling the environment and creating a one-world government. Unfortunately, they have succeeded in so many of their endeavors. We are the Babylon of the modern world in many ways. Gloria Steinem, in a *Saturday Review* article in March of 1973, stated that by the year 2000 "we will, I hope, raise our children to believe in human potential and not in God." And we wonder why prayer and Bible reading and the Ten Commandments and creation science have no place in the education of America's young minds? What happened in Babylon has been repeated today in America. Our young people find themselves in the same culture in which Daniel lived in his day.

How could this happen in America? It happened the same way in Babylon. These were planned techniques designed to gradually change a young person's conscience, values, and behavior. We have taught a generation of young people that they have a right to develop their own personal values apart from their parental influences or authorities. We have convinced a generation that there is no right from wrong and that there are no moral absolutes nor moral truths. "Tolerance" is the buzzword of this generation.

Daniel walked in this same world but he did not give in. He was resistant. How? It was not because his parents protested or picketed. They obviously did the best thing parents can do for their children. They trained him in the way he should go (Prov. 22:6). We should find it interesting that Daniel did not say "no" to a Babylonian education. He knew how to handle it. He had parents who had built something into him. They named him "God is my judge," Daniel. They taught him and instilled values in him.

Christian parents seeking to raise children to live in a 21st century Babylonian culture in America should not think they can leave it to the school nor the church to instill these values. We should dispense with the notion that "it takes a village" to raise a child. No, it takes a mom or a dad to train these precious lives in the way that they should go. When we leave it to the village they will pull our kids down every time! Daniel could not change the influences around him but he did have control over his reaction to these influences. Daniel *purposed in his heart.* (Dan. 1:8) Even though he was learning a new language and a new literature and a new lifestyle he drew the line when it came to eating the king's meat. He had a biblical admonition regarding this. He purposed in his heart not to do it. Here was a young man who would not compromise.

We should find it interesting that there's no attempt on Daniel's part to separate himself from the culture around him. Daniel was no isolationist as some are today. He was capable of interacting with the pagan culture around him without being contaminated by it. We should know that we will never be salt and light and influence our culture if we're totally isolated from it. Daniel actually learned from his culture. He compared it to what he understood from God's point of view. What we need today is what Daniel had — that is, a knowledge and perception of what is biblical and what is not. Part of the problem with our own pagan culture is that the church has retreated from it for years. Some of us have given in to it and given up on it. Then, very subtly in place of influencing it, the culture began to influence the church, so much so that we are hard pressed to see the biblical pattern of the church we find in Acts in many modern churches today.

Look at Daniel. He went along with the teaching because he already knew what he believed. He went along with the name change because he knew that they could change his name but not his heart. But Daniel drew the line when it came to "eating the king's meat." Now, one would think it might be just the opposite — that is, that he would go along with something like food and say no to the name change. On the surface, had you asked me, I might have advised him to stay away from the literature, to not pollute his mind with the godless morals of the pagan ideas. Why did Daniel say yes to the education but no to the food? He drew the line on what the Word of God said. There's no strict prohibition to taking a different name or learning what others believe. However, in that Jewish dispensation there was a strong prohibition about what Jews could eat. Not only was Nebuchadnezzar's food not kosher, it had been offered to idols. Daniel did not refuse the king's meat because he was a vegetarian or a dietary fanatic. He obeyed the Word of God. He took his stand upon the Word of God.

One of the reasons so many of us fall into our own world culture is that we do not know what the Bible says and thus we compromise and assimilate ourselves into the culture with no real convictions. Seldom do we "purpose in our hearts" so that when the time comes and we have to make a decision, we've already made it in our heart and mind. Daniel was just a teenager at this time. Most of life's major decisions are made in our youth. Decisions regarding our careers, our marriages, our friends, our habits, even decisions of trusting Christ are made when we are young. Daniel had made his decision long before he got to Babylon. He "purposed in his heart" to stand upon the Word of God. Daniel did not wait until he got to an intersection of life to decide which way he would turn. He had already made his mind up before he got there.

What are the criteria we should use in our culture today to determine which activities to engage in and which not? Some would say peer pressure. For Daniel it was the Word of God. He set his mind. He purposed in his heart. Life is full of intersections and compromise is the name of the game in our culture today. It is the American way of life. Daniel is saying to us across these centuries, "Don't give in, be resistant."

What about us? We are going out this week into a world that seems to be out of control. What are we going to do? We are all under pressure to conform to the culture, to give in. Daniel was under incredible pressure himself. Everything changed around him. His language changed. What he was reading changed. His diet changed. His name changed. The names of his friends changed. Babylon was trying to squeeze him into its mold so he would look like the rest of them, talk like the rest of them, act like the rest of them, dress like the rest of them, eat like the rest of them, be like the rest of them. It was a decisive and deliberate attempt to cut him off from his own culture and his own religious roots. The same thing is happening in America today. When we open our eyes we see it plainly. There is so much pressure to conform to the culture. Learn from Daniel. Purpose in your heart to draw the line at the Word of God. We belong to the family of God. We have our own culture, our own language, our own literature, our own lifestyle, and our own loyalties. When we look around and our world looks out of control, remember that Daniel reminds us it was "the Lord" who gave Jehoiakim into Nebuchadnezzar's hand. God is in control. So what should we do? We should take Daniel's advice. "Don't give in…be resistant." Dare to be a Daniel, dare to stand alone, dare to have a firm purpose, and dare to make it known!

Chapter 2

Don't give up...be consistent

Dan. 1:8-16

Often the tendency of so many of us is to be overcome and overrun by the culture around us. For some it becomes easier to simply give up trying to hold on to biblical principles and go along with the culture. If Daniel is saying anything to us across these centuries he is challenging us to not give up and to be consistent. Daniel was a young man who would not compromise and would not quit. Daniel stated to the chief of the eunuchs that he *would not defile himself* by eating the King's unkosher meat. (Dan. 1:8) His boss was reluctant but Daniel was determined. He would not give up, he remained consistent. Finally, his boss "consented" to a test to see if Daniel's diet would suffice.

The single characteristic of those who succeed in the challenges of life is this element of consistency. Joseph, in an

Egyptian dungeon, did not give up. Paul, in a Philippian jail, did not give up. Daniel, in Babylonian captivity, did not give up. And God did not forget any of them.

So often in a culture that is crumbling like ours we're tempted to ask, "Where is God?" He was there with Daniel and He is here with us. Note the quote, *And the Lord gave Jehoiakim king of Judah into his hand.* (Dan. 1:2) Note that *God had brought Daniel into the favor and goodwill of the chief of the eunuchs.* (Dan. 1:9) Note that God gave them *knowledge and skill in all literature and wisdom.* (Dan. 1:17). God was in control of every one of Daniel's circumstances and situations.

I love what the Bible says in Daniel 1:9, *Now God had brought Daniel into the favor and goodwill of the chief of the eunuchs.* When we establish standards like Daniel, God shows up on our side. Daniel had *purposed in his heart.* Daniel had made his choice. Daniel had set his mind. In the very next verse we find God intervening. It was not Daniel's stand that influenced the chief of the eunuchs, it was God Himself. Remember, God has the remote control in His hand. He can turn us up or turn us off. He can change our channel or mute us if He so desires. He is in control.

Many are prone to give up what they stand for when they're out in the culture. Some of us seem to be geared to think that if we do not compromise we might lose our position or even our promotion. Daniel had figured out who he wanted on his side. It was not his boss, it was his God. He knew the truth of Proverbs 16:7, *When a man's ways please the Lord, He makes even his enemies to be at peace with him.*

So, what is the point? If we're going somewhere in life we need to learn some lessons from our friend Daniel. Don't play politics. We should live our lives in such a way that they line up with the Word of God and please him in the process. And then we can watch Him work on those around us as he did in Daniel's day. It is not enough to simply be resistant if we're not consistent. Some start well but give up and go with the crowd around them.

Oh that we could grasp Daniel's spirit. He *purposed in his heart*. This is not a guy trying to prove something to someone with a bunch of self-righteousness. This was no show. This was from his heart. There are some who don't give in and are resistant but who become caustic and crude when trying to resist a culture. The Bible reminds us that a soft answer turns away wrath. Daniel has a disarming way about him that honors God. He not only calls upon us saying "Don't give in, be resistant," but he challenges us by saying, "Don't give up, be consistent!"

Chapter 3

Don't give out...be persistent

Dan. 1:17-21

I love those words in Daniel 1:21 — *Thus Daniel continued*. He finished strongly! He was persistent. For 70 years he did not give in, nor did he give up, nor did he give out. He was not only resistant but also consistent and persistent. He outlived Nebuchadnezzar and he even outlived Nebuchadnezzar's empire. Daniel lived into the days of Cyrus the ruler of the Medes and Persians, and God used him to make a tremendous difference in his culture and in his world.

When we do not give in nor give up nor give out God will bless. Note that He will give protection. *God had brought Daniel into the favor and goodwill of the chief of the eunuchs*. (Dan. 1:9) God has His own ways of watching over His own when they are faithful to His word and obedient to His will. It is a wonderful thing in a crumbling culture to know that God has the controls in His own hand. He also gives knowledge. *God gave them knowledge and skill in all literature and wisdom.* (Dan. 1:17). At the end of three years Daniel took his oral exams. He flew through to the head of the class. He applied himself, he prepared, and God blessed him. Preparing intellectually is a requirement for living in our Babylon. Like Daniel, we do not live in Jerusalem any longer. For example, who would have thought we would ever have to ask if it was okay to see a Walt Disney film? As was true in Daniel's day, truth is on our side. We, like him, can live uncompromising lives. We, like Daniel, can stand true to the Word of God. We should not let anyone in the king's court tempt us to compromise and the Lord will raise us up before our peers as He did Daniel. Promotion does not come from the east nor the west but from the Lord.

God will also give us influence. The Bible says, *Thus Daniel continued until the first year of King Cyrus*. When we read these words in Daniel 1:21 we find that this has covered a span of 70 years. What an influence Daniel had. He not only did not give in, he did not give up, and he did not give out. When Cyrus made a decree that allowed the Jews to return to Jerusalem, Daniel had a part in that. When Nehemiah went back to be the rebuilder of the broken walls, Daniel had a part in that. When Ezra went back to re-establish the book of the law Daniel had a part in that. And 500 years later when the wise men made their way to Bethlehem from the East, if you will look back far enough you will find Daniel behind that too. Those Magi knew about a Messiah because their ancestors had heard through the uncompromising life of a young Hebrew captive in Babylon by the name of Daniel.

Yes, *Daniel continued.* And God gave him protection, wisdom, and influence along the way. This should be a tremendous encouragement to all of us who are seeking to address a 21st century Babylonian culture in the western world. It would be wonderful if it were said of us that we too "continued," that we did not give in nor give up nor give out, that we too were resistant, consistent, and persistent.

In 1992 our First Baptist Church of Dallas high school choir had the wonderful privilege of ministering during the Summer Olympics in Barcelona, Spain. Those of us who remember those Olympic games have forever etched in our minds the 400-meter run. The favorite to win the gold medal was a young man by the name of Derek Redmond. Derek was 26-years-old. In the middle of his race Derek Redmond fell flat on the track. When he fought his way back to his feet he grabbed the back of his leg in pain. A torn hamstring had brought a lifetime of dreams to a miserable end in a split second. But Derek Redmond got up. He began hopping around the track on one leg. When he reached the home stretch a large man broke through the security guards and onto the track. He was wearing a tee shirt that said, "Have you hugged your kid today?" The man put his arms around Derek Redmond and together they hobbled toward the finish line. That man, it turned out, was Derek Redmond's father, Jim Redmond. It made for a beautiful picture. There was a fallen hero and a loving father making sure that he finished strongly. And anyone who watched on television that day will never forget that scene.

Derek Redmond is a picture of some of us. Some of us are lying on the track of life with our dreams smashed and our hopes dashed. Setbacks are no fun. But look, from out of the stands comes a loving father who takes our arm and puts it over his own shoulder. He'll see us to the finish line if we will walk with him! Like Derek Redmond we have a hope. Don't give out, be persistent.

In every one of these verses in Daniel 1 we see God is not removed from the events of human history. He is not sitting in a rocking chair somewhere with His hands folded, twiddling His thumbs on some distant planet. He is here. And, He is holding the controls! He can turn you on or turn you off at His will. He can quiet you or let you be heard at His own will. I know brilliant men like Daniel who had it all going for them but they gave in and God turned their volume down so that no one hears them anymore. I know others for whom He pushed the mute button and still others where He turned them off completely. I know others He's turning back up and putting back in service. He's going to use them again for His glory. He holds the remote control in His own hand. He was not only active behind the scenes in Daniel's day but in ours as well. No wonder Daniel is saying, "Don't give out, be persistent."

We live in a world today much like Daniel's. Ours, too, is a world that is out of control. We're living in a culture that is increasingly opposed to what we believe. We live in a culture that is busy at work with a plan to re-educate our young minds. We don't call it *Babylonianism* but that's what it is and it is all around us.

Daniel *purposed in his heart.* (Dan. 1:8). And *Daniel continued.* (Dan. 1:21). Daniel lived to see the fall of that pagan empire. Daniel's God is our God! He has not changed nor has His word. Could it be that He's simply waiting on some of us to *purpose in our hearts and continue*? Could it be that He's waiting on some of us to stop giving in and giving up and giving out. He is at work behind the scenes and is in control.

What does this mean for us today? Simply because God is in control does not mean that Daniel was passive and did nothing. He worked, he prayed, he took a stand, he studied, he influenced others. Yes, God is in control but He desires and expects our own obedience. Daniel made a choice. He purposed in his heart. God did not make the choice for him. His friends Shadrach, Meshach, and Abednego did not make the choice for him. He purposed in his own heart. The same is true for us. Life is about making right choices.

Daniel is saying to us today that we, too, can make it! How? By deciding which way we're going to turn before we ever get to the intersection. Along the way we hear him saying, "Don't give in, be resistant." Our tendency tomorrow is simply to give in to the culture, to go its way, but we must not. We must "purpose in our own heart" and draw a line with the Word of God.

We can also hear him saying, "Don't give up, be consistent." Our tendency tomorrow is to be so overwhelmed that we give up and lay down our biblical principles and conform to the culture. We can also hear him saying, "Don't give out be persistent." Our tendency is so often to simply quit the race — but we're called upon to finish strongly. I love those words in Daniel 1:21, *And Daniel continued.*

Are there any of my readers who seek to control your own life? You hold the remote control in your own hand seeking to control everything around you — your volume, your brightness, and your contrast. Give the remote control back to Him today. Say, "Lord, here it is. You control my life." And then, "purpose in your heart" to continue. Daniel's God is our God. "Don't give out, be persistent!"

Part Two

Real video — Back to the future

One of my good friends is Byron Forrester. Byron has lived in Dallas all of his life but he is not a Cowboys fan. He is the world's biggest Green Bay Packers fan and with good reason. His dad, Bill, was an All-Pro linebacker on the great world championship teams of yesteryear in Green Bay. Consequently, Byron had a major interest in a recent Super Bowl which was won by Green Bay. He videotaped the game and, when I asked him a few days afterwards, he indicated he'd watched the tape 14 times!

As I prepared to write this chapter on Daniel 2, I thought about Byron Forrester watching that video of the Super Bowl so many times in the aftermath of his team's victory. However, I thought how interesting it would be if he had had the video before the game was actually played. Think about that. Suppose you had the video of the game before it was played? Let's imagine that you watched it several times before the Super Bowl and knew how it was going to end. You knew what events and what major plays would lead up to the final whistle to end the game. Then, just suppose you went to the game and sat in the stands with your friends and fans. The game moves into the fourth quarter. It is not looking good for your team. But you're not concerned. You've already seen the video. You know what is coming next. The people around you start wringing their hands and stomping their feet and throwing down their hats and yelling at the referee at the top of their lungs. But you just sit there and smile.

Wouldn't that be something? Well, that is exactly what happens in Daniel Chapter 2. God shows us the video of the Super Bowl of world history. He lets us see how our world culture and world history play out the final game. He takes us through the fourth quarter and all the way to the end. He also lets us see that we win in the end and all of this takes place before it actually happens!

It is amazing to me that more of us do not watch this video in Daniel Chapter 2. The events of September 11, 2001, have caused consternation and concern on the parts of many. Some people around us are wringing their hands. Others are worried. Some are stomping their feet and yelling at the top of their lungs. We who have seen the video and have gone "back to the future" can smile. Why? Because God provides for us in this one chapter of Scripture the whole game of human history and reveals to us how it ends in victory for His side. This is important knowledge to have for those learning how to stand in a culture around us that is running contrary to our convictions and principles. We seem to be in the fourth quarter and things are not looking good. But when we read Daniel Chapter 2 we see the final result before it ever happens!

The second chapter of Daniel is one of the most amazing chapters in all the Bible. Here is a man by the name of Daniel who lived 2,500 years ago and he not only tells us in detail what has ensued in world history over the last 2,500 years but what is happening in our world today. The key to understanding this chapter of Scripture is found in a few key phrases in Daniel 2:28-29, 45. He begins by informing us that *there is a God in heaven who reveals secrets.* He goes on to say that this God has made known *what will be in latter days...what will come to pass after this...what will be in the future.* This chapter with its image of the statue and the stone deals with events that had not yet happened when Daniel penned those words. It is like watching the Super Bowl video before the game has been played. This chapter is prophetic in nature. Daniel tells us how world history will end. And as the verses of this chapter unfold before us we find that we could very well be living in the days that are, in fact, the beginning of the end. He reminds us in verse 45 that *the dream is certain and its interpretation is sure.*

The first 30 verses of the second chapter of Daniel are mostly narrative in nature. The chapter begins with King Nebuchadnezzar having a terrible nightmare. All of us have had experiences when we've had a dream which we could either not remember or could not figure out what it meant. This is what happened to Nebuchadnezzar. In his dream he saw a great statue and then a great stone. The stone smashed the statue on its feet and brought the whole statue crumbling to earth. Then in Nebuchadnezzar's dream the stone filled the entire earth.

Being troubled by this dream the king calls together all of his wise men. Here was a convocation that was a new age who's who. They all came and stood before the king. He gathered together the magicians and astrologers and sorcerers and reminded them that they got paid for being wise and instructed them to tell him what he dreamed and what it meant. They could not do it. So Nebuchadnezzar orders the whole lot of them to be put to death. Incidentally, Daniel and his three friends, Shadrach, Meshach, and Abednego, were included in this dilemma.

When Daniel hears about the king's decree he gets his friends together not to plot but to pray. He gets them in a prayer meeting and the result was that *the secret was revealed to Daniel in a night vision.* (Dan. 2:19) Next, Daniel goes before Nebuchadnezzar and lays it all out before him. He stands before the king and says, *There's a God in heaven who reveals secrets and He has made known to King Nebuchadnezzar what will be in the latter days.* (Dan. 2:28) This is an important reminder for those of us who are seeking to engage a crumbling culture around us in a 21st century world. Yes, *there is a God in heaven who reveals secrets.* Like Daniel, we, too, live in a culture that is increasingly hostile to what we believe and hold dear to our own hearts. But there is a God in heaven! Yes, our children have pressures and temptations most of us knew nothing about in our own adolescence. But there is a God in heaven! Yes, we are indeed confronted in the marketplace daily by those who have far different moral values than do we. But, there is a God in heaven!

The rest of the second chapter of Daniel deals with the interpretation of Nebuchadnezzar's dream along with its meaning and application for us today in our 21st century world. When we take the Book of Daniel and lay along side it our world history textbooks and today's newspaper we see that the Word of God is true and it is as much alive today as ever. These three things, the Book of Daniel, the world history text, and today's newspaper reveal to us what God is saying as we seek to engage our culture.

It is important to remember that Daniel is teaching us how to live in the midst of and how to engage a pagan culture around us. In the first chapter he has shown us the importance of not giving in nor giving up nor giving out. Now, in Chapter 2, he provides us with a panorama of world history to assure us that we're on the winning side even in days when victory seems somewhat remote. There's a hunger in the human heart to be a part of something that makes a difference, something that is enduring, something that is permanent. And this is exactly what Chapter 2 of Daniel does for us. It provides us with the confidence when we enter the marketplace of culture that we're the ones who are going to truly win in the end. We can see the video played out before the actual event takes place. We can enjoy the game of life with a lot less fear and tension when we understand the truth of Daniel Chapter 2. In fact, because Daniel himself knew this fact he lived the rest of his life without giving in, without giving up, and without giving out.

As we confront our own culture today God reveals two very important things to us which give us confidence and courage to go on. God reveals to us the scope of human history with a statue. He also reveals to us the hope of human history with a stone. Let's hasten on to look at these truths and learn from them as we seek advice from Daniel in addressing our own culture.

Chapter 4

God reveals the scope of human history with a statue

Dan. 2:31-43

If you could pick one spot in all the world to go and sit for a few minutes, where would you go? I would not have to give it a second thought. For me it would be the summit of the Mount of Olives. When one sits there atop the Mount of Olives and looks over the Kidron Valley, he sees one of the most beautiful panoramas in all the world. It was from that spot that the Psalmist said that Jerusalem was *beautiful in its loftiness, the joy of the whole earth.* (Ps. 48:2) As you view the panorama from left to right, on a clear day you can see the mountains of Bethlehem. Next is the beauty of Mount Zion with the Tower of David. Straight ahead and across the valley is Mount Moriah. There one can view the pinnacle of the Temple and the Temple Mount itself where once stood the glory of Solomon's Temple and where now resides what is commonly referred to as the Dome of the Rock. The old walled city of Jerusalem is before you and the eastern gate is in plain sight. Looking toward the north and up through the Kidron Valley one sees Mount Scopus and beyond that mountain on another more distant mountaintop is the tomb of Samuel the prophet. It is an incredible panorama.

When we come to the second chapter of Daniel we stand on a tall mountaintop of Scripture. We see the panorama of world history encompassing what Luke calls *the times of the Gentiles*. (Luke 21:24) This involves the time from 605 B.C. until the consummation of this age and the return of our Lord Jesus Christ himself as King of kings and Lord of lords. God himself stepped into the dream of an ancient Babylonian king in order to reveal your future. He reveals to us the scope of human history with a statue. Therefore, it behooves us to ask several questions as we deal with these verses of Scripture.

The first question is "what?" What did Nebuchadnezzar dream? What did Daniel see in the interruption? What is this statue that's revealed to us in Daniel 2:31-33? Daniel says it was a great statue that was made of gold, silver, bronze, iron, and clay. Can you picture it? Twice we read the word "great" in describing it. It was an awesome image. The statue was that of the image of a man. The head was of gold. The chest and arms were of silver. The abdomen was of bronze. The legs were of iron. The feet and toes were a mixture of both iron and clay. The statue was to have a limited lifetime. Its destiny was destruction. This destruction came suddenly, surely, and swiftly. A great stone demolished it and then that particular stone filled the earth.

Next we come to the "who" question. We find this addressed in Daniel 2:36-43. Who is this statue? Who does it reveal? Anyone who has studied world history from 600 B.C. to the present day will tell you there have been four world empires. The Babylonian Empire began in 605 B.C. In 539 B.C. the Medes and the Persians of the great Medeo-Persian Empire diverted the Euphrates River, entered the great walled city of Babylon by night, and Babylonia fell after only 65 years of world dominance. Next, in 331 B.C. a young Greek, Alexander, swept across the world of his day and Greece ruled the world. Then, in 146 B.C. the Roman legions began their conquest of the world by crushing everything and everyone in their path. All these world empires were pictured in Nebuchadnezzar's dream, and centuries before they came into being. The Bible is indeed a miracle book.

Daniel says that the head of this statue was made of gold (Dan. 2:37-38). Who is this head of gold? There is no question about this. The Bible is explicitly clear in Daniel 2:37-38. Babylon herself is this head of gold. Babylon was known for its gold. Herodotus, the historian, visited Babylon a century after Nebuchadnezzar and writes that he never saw such a proliferation of gold. There were golden temples and golden altars and golden walkways. Nebuchadnezzar built a golden city with a golden throne. How do we know this head of gold is the picture of the Babylonian Empire? It is not some way out speculation. It is not my own idea. The Bible explicitly says it. Daniel stood before Nebuchadnezzar and said, *you are that head of gold.* (Daniel 2:38). However, the world empire known as Babylon fell after just a few score years. But before it fell God revealed its demise.

Note the *chest and arms of silver.* (Dan. 2:32) Who is this chest of silver? Unquestionably it is the Medeo-Persian Empire. Daniel reveals to Nebuchadnezzar that *after you* shall arise another kingdom (Dan. 2:39). Any student of world history can tell you that it was, in fact, the Medes and the Persians who defeated the Babylonian's supremacy and became the world empire and the world power under Cyrus. There's no doubt about the identity of this kingdom represented by silver. When Daniel later interprets the writing on the wall at the feast of Belshazzar he says, *Your kingdom has been divided, and given to the Medes and Persians.* (Dan. 5:28) Thus the Babylonian Empire was no more and never will be again! It gave way to the Medeo-Persian Empire. This Empire is mentioned by name in Daniel 8:20-21. History verifies these empires and we need not go outside of Scripture to find out who they are. From the Book of Esther we learned that these Persian rulers would rule over all the earth. The two arms of the coalition are the Medes and the Persians who coalesced into one great world empire. This is not speculation. It is the Word of God that has been validated in world history. History has recorded that it happened just as Daniel had predicted.

Note next the *abdomen of bronze.* (Dan. 2:32) Who is this kingdom of bronze? It is Greece. How do we know? The

Greeks defeated the Medes and the Persians in 334 B.C. Alexander the Great took the throne of Greece at the age of 20. He defeated the Persians and then began his conquest of the known world. He died at the age of 32 weeping because there were no more worlds to conquer! We also know that this third great world empire of Nebuchadnezzar's dream was Greece because God identified this kingdom by name also in Daniel 8:21 and Daniel 11:2. The Greeks were known for their bronze and their brass. Greek soldiers wore helmets of brass, breastplates of brass, and carried shields of brass. They carried swords of brass. Brass was the symbol of the Greek conquest during the days of the empire under Alexander the Great.

Greece ruled the world and a number of its citizens who lived during this period made contributions that we enjoy today. Herodotus stands without peer as the father of historians. Hippocrates is the father of modern medicine. The Greek philosophers Socrates, Plato, and Aristotle helped formulate mindsets for centuries. We know that this third world empire is Greece not only because world history played out the fact but also because God said it. Just as Daniel had predicted in the interruption of the dream, the Medeo-Persian Empire that crushed Babylon was conquered by Greece. The amazing thing is that it was all laid out in the Book of Daniel scores of years before it happened. It is like watching a video of the Super Bowl before it is ever played!

Next note the *legs of iron*. (Dan. 2:33) Who are these legs of iron? There is little if any doubt about this. Here we see the great Roman Empire. Rome followed the Greeks in world dominion. Every history book tells us this. However, the Bible tells us this fact hundreds of years before it happened. This is real video. This is going "back to the future." This is watching the game before it has ever been played.

The Roman Empire dominated the world for centuries because it ruled with such an iron hand. It was ruthless. It broke in pieces and crushed others (see Daniel 2:40). Iron was the symbol of strength. Every schoolchild has studied the iron legions of Rome. Even when our Lord Jesus Christ was born in Bethlehem we remember that the Bible says that *a decree went out from Caesar Augustus that all the world should be registered.* (Luke 2:1) Rome ruled the world upon the collapse of Greek dominance.

Daniel foresees the great Roman Empire being divided in Daniel 2:41. Students of world history know that in fact the Roman Empire was indeed divided. Rome is represented by the two legs of the statue. The divided Empire was centered in Rome in the West and in Constantinople, modern day Istanbul, in the East. This became the great Byzantine Empire, which colonized the world to the north and to the east, into Russia in the north and the Middle East to the east. From Rome the western part of the Empire colonized the West and spread through Europe. The monarchies of France, Germany, Spain, and Great Britain were the result of the western spread of the Roman Empire. Every single nation of the Western Hemisphere was begun by one of the nations of the Roman Empire. Our own western world is Roman at its roots. It is imprinted upon our own history. We have a senate. We got that from Rome. We have a representative form of government. Our courts, our laws, our military all reflect the Roman Empire. In the east the iron leg of the Roman Empire reached into Russia. They called their ruler the czar, which is the Russian spelling for Caesar. In the west the German rulers were called Kaisers, which is the German spelling of Caesar. The Roman Caesars influence our world to the very present day.

Rome did not collapse because another world power defeated her. She collapsed from within. Anyone who has read the history of the Roman Empire has seen the moral decay that brought about the collapse of Rome. Even though the Roman Empire as a political entity has long since died, many of its institutions and ideals still live on in our western world.

In Daniel 7:7 these four metals are seen again as beast of prey. The horn is the symbol of ruling power. This corresponds with the ten toes of Daniel 2. In Daniel 7:21-22 this fourth world kingdom is to continue "until" the Second Coming of Christ. This could only be Rome. But how? How could the Roman Empire continue until today?

The answer to this question is found in the feet and toes of iron and clay which are revealed in Daniel 2:42-43. History has verified the accuracy of all Daniel's predictions. All four world empires are revealed in Daniel in the order of their conquest. And, this revelation came before most of them even existed! The greatest proof we have that the Bible is true is the way prophecy has been fulfilled throughout its pages. There has never been a world empire in the sense of Rome since she ruled the world. Now, there have been many men and many nations who set out to be. There were men like Napoleon and Stalin and Hitler and Saddam Hussein and Osama bin Laden. Men and nations for centuries have plotted and planned and boasted. Some have even slaughtered millions in attempts to set up a fifth world empire but all have failed.

But when we look carefully at the statue revealed through Daniel's interpretation of Nebuchadnezzar's dream, we find that there is one more part of the statue, the feet and toes of iron and clay. Who are these toes? They represent the continuation of Rome. In the end times the Bible reveals that a federation of nations rising out of the ruins of the Roman Empire will emerge. They will seek to mix the iron and the clay, that is, the ideas of totalitarianism and imperialism and the principles of democracy, which are pliable and can be molded like clay. However, they simply do not blend together. Democracy may not be the best form of government. Theocracy may well be the best form. Democracy alone is not what made America great. The Bible reveals to us that it is *righteousness which exalts a nation*. (Prov. 14:34)

It is of note that Daniel's prophecy passes over a period of time from Rome and the first coming of Christ to the return of Jesus Christ. This is more commonly referred to as the Church Age. Why is it not addressed in Daniel? It is not surprising that there should be an interlude here. The Old Testament never saw the Church Age. Paul himself wrote in Greek that it was a *musterion*, that is, a sacred secret, a mystery. Daniel 7:15-25 throws considerable light on the identification of these nations. In the last days these nations will rise out of the ruins of the old Roman Empire. Revelation Chapter 17 talks about 10 kings. They talk about a one-world government. Out of these nations will one day arise an electrifying leader who will promise to free the world from war and economic problems. This electrifying world leader, more commonly referred to as the Antichrist, has gained a new sense of popularity from the *Left Behind* book series of Tim LaHaye and Jerry B. Jenkins.

More and more people believe we are seeing this before our very eyes in the European Common Market. Could they be the coalition of iron and clay, the political and economic union? Until recently this coalition appeared impossible. Europe was divided from the east to the west, but almost overnight the Berlin Wall fell. The pieces of the prophetic puzzle began falling into place. Then the Soviet Union collapsed. Now Israel is back in the land. Europe has moved to a common currency. These are major steps in the European coalition. The stage seems to be being set and the props are being put in place for the return of our Lord. When I continue to hear talk of one world government my ears perk up. When I see Israel miraculously back in the land after centuries of dispersion I open my eyes a little wider. When I see the European community rising and coming together I take particular note. And then when I read Daniel I'm reminded that he has told us all of this two and a half millennia ago.

Thus, in this statue, God reveals to us the scope of human history. There have only been four world empires. World history has verified all that Daniel prophesied. And, that which is yet to happen will be fulfilled just as all the others have also. We have the video before the big game is even played out!

It is interesting to note that the statue diminished from the head to the foot. Look at it carefully. It is obviously top-heavy and weak in the feet. We see an amazing thing here. We see the downward digression of human existence. Note these are deteriorating qualities. That is, gold to silver to bronze to iron to mud and finally to clay. The image is top-heavy. It is weakest in its feet. This strongly suggested the degeneration of the human race through the ages. This truth is diametrically opposite to the evolutionist who seeks to interrupt human history. Instead of man beginning as dust from nothing and ascending to gold, God reveals to us in the Word that man in the time of the Gentiles begins as gold and degenerates in the end to nothing but mud. Every human man-made empire has gone this way.

This principle of deterioration of civilization is obvious. We are not getting better. We're getting worse. Before our very eyes we're witnessing the demise of the Christian culture and a Christian civilization in the West. This deterioration is seen all around us. We're witnessing the demise of a culture. We're not getting better. Darwinian thought says we're progressing upward. His philosophy tells us we rise from mud and clay to gold. But God says just the opposite.

Even though we may be watching the deterioration of our society, it is not time for disappointment or despair. God has a plan. And this plan is about to take place. God reveals the scope of human history in this statue.

Next we come to another question. It is the "why" question. Why this statute? What Nebuchadnezzar dreamed and what Daniel revealed was, in the words of the Lord Jesus, the *times of the Gentiles*. (Luke 21:24) Our Lord himself tells here of the dispersion of Israel in the times of the Gentiles when Jerusalem will be trodden down. The *times of the Gentiles* is that time between Nebuchadnezzar and the second coming of the Lord Jesus Christ when the kingdom of Israel is in abeyance.

God had commended the government of the world to Israel. It was to be administered by priests and prophets and godly kings. But unfortunately, Israel disobeyed. Thus God brought forth an intermission and for an interlude gave the governments of the world to the Gentiles. Remember that the Bible says, *the Lord gave Jehoiakim king of Judah into Nebuchadnezzar's hand*. (Dan. 1:2) This "time of the Gentiles" has been going on since the days of Nebuchadnezzar. From 605 B.C. until the present day the chosen people of God have been scattered over the earth. This period corresponds with the days of human history when Israel was without a king. Hosea says, *For the children of Israel shall abide many days without king or prince, without sacrifice or sacred pillar, without ephod or teraphim. Afterward the children of Israel shall return and seek the Lord their God and David their king. They shall fear the Lord and His goodness in the latter days*. (Hos. 3:4-5). Our world is winding down. When all is hopelessly lost King Jesus will return! He will end the time of the Gentiles, establish anew from Israel His kingdom and rule for a millennium of perfect peace. Yes, this statue in Daniel 2 shows us the scope of human history.

The stage is being set today. Many of the major props have been put in place during my own lifetime. Israel is back in her land. This prop was put in place in 1948. Another important prop came in 1967 when for the first time since the days of Nebuchadnezzar Israel controlled the City of Jerusalem. Something dramatic is going on in Europe at the present time. The coalition of iron and clay is coming together in an economic and political manner. Until recently this seemed to be impossible. Who would have thought we would have seen the fall of the Soviet Union and the fall of the Berlin Wall seemingly overnight?

Even though Israel is back in her land she is still under the times of the Gentiles. Ask the Jews if they feel the burden of Gentile oppression. It is constantly poured out on them from the United Nations. And the holy city of Jerusalem herself has a constant reminder of this fact. I wish I could walk you through the Dung Gate into the Temple Mount today. Look at any picture of Jerusalem and what do you see? A golden dome on Mount Moriah. The Mosque of Omar is the third holiest Moslem site. On the holy Temple Mount is a Muslim mosque and today Islam controls the Temple Mount in the very heart of Jerusalem herself. The Jews may have successfully raided Entebbe and may have won the Six-Day War against insurmountable odds. But, they have never touched the Temple Mount. If they did we would see World War III. When Prime Minister Ariel Sharon stepped upon the Temple Mount at the turn of the millennium it brought about a new *intifadeh* that resulted in the deaths of hundreds and hundreds of Jews and Palestinians alike. Yes, Israel is still under Gentile domination and will be until the *times of the Gentiles* are fulfilled.

Our world seems to be standing at the brink of something catastrophic. Rogue nations with possible nuclear weapons have the capacity to annihilate millions. At this writing we're engaged in a new war on terrorism. Sophisticated terrorists are waging this new war and many believe it is just a matter of time before one of them unleashes a nuclear arsenal of some type. God is allowing man to run his course. Man is showing his true colors. He is set to destroy his world and civilization. This is true economically, materially, biologically, meteorologically, and virtually in every way. It is going to get worse before it gets better. And just when it looks as though there's no hope left, our Lord Jesus Christ will return. The uncut stone will end the time of the Gentiles and fill the earth with His own glorious kingdom. We have the video before us and God reveals to us the scope of human history in this statue.

How will it all end? When will it all end? History seems to be reaching its climax. We are winding down. The Bible says, "When you see all these things coming to pass lift up your eyes for your redemption draws near."

What does this have to do with us as we seek to engage the culture around us? It has for us the same effect it had on Daniel. He reminds us that God is in control. We can trust him. Everything thus far has unfolded just as Nebuchadnezzar dreamed and as Daniel revealed and that which is left to be fulfilled will follow suit. We have seen the video before the end of the game. As we confront our culture we do not have to give in nor give up nor give out. We can have the same confidence of Daniel. That is, that God is in control. He reveals the scope of human history to us with a statue. And, we win in the end!

Chapter 5

God reveals the hope of human history with a stone

Dan. 2:34-35; 44-45

In the words of Daniel, *the dream is certain, and its interpretation is sure*. (Dan. 2:45) There is coming a day when this stone cut without human hands will smite the statue at its feet, at the time of this coming confederacy of nations. This will cause it to come crumbling down, revealing the end of the world as we have known it. Then, this stone grows into a great mountain that fills the earth revealing to us the coming kingdom of God that stands forever! Once again we must ask ourselves some questions.

First, we come to the "who" question. Who is this stone that we read about in Daniel Chapter 2? Let's let the Scripture tell us. *The stone, which the builders rejected, has become the chief cornerstone.* (Ps. 118:22) *He will be as a sanctuary, but a stone of stumbling and a rock of offense to both the houses of Israel.* (Isa. 8:14) To Israel the Lord Jesus Christ was a stone of stumbling because He came the first time in the form of a servant (Isa. 53). He came on a donkey and not a stallion. As a stone he was rejected by the Jewish builders. The Lord says, *The stone which the builders rejected has become the chief cornerstone.* (Matt. 21:42) He went on to say, *On whomever this stone falls it will ground him to powder.* (Matt. 21:44) Thus we ask ourselves as we read Daniel 2:34, who is this stone? It is none other than our Lord Jesus Christ himself!

Daniel says that this stone was *cut out without hands.* (Dan. 2:34) That is, it was supernatural in origin. Neither human hands nor human means brought it into existence. The Lord Jesus Christ was there in the beginning. When he came to this earth he clothed himself in human flesh. No human made that happen. He was virgin born. He was the stone "cut without human hands." The stone that strikes the great statue of King Nebuchadnezzar's dream is none other than our Lord Jesus himself. This stone is the hope of all of human history.

Next we come to the "what" question. What is this event that takes place in Daniel 2? This stone hitting the statue is the second coming of our Lord Jesus. Our Lord will return in great power and glory. Handel's masterpiece only revealed what John the Revelator said on Patmos, *The kingdoms of this world have become the kingdoms of our Lord and of His Christ, and He shall reign forever and ever.* (Rev. 11:15) The great fact of Bible prophesy is that the Lord Jesus Christ is returning visibly, bodily, and personally to this earth. Palm Sunday was not the last journey our Lord will make down the Mount of Olives and across the Kidron Valley and through the Eastern Gate. He is coming back and will not be riding on a donkey but upon a white stallion. He will not come as a suffering servant but He will come as the King of all kings and the Lord of all lords. *He should strike the nations. And He Himself will rule them with a rod of iron.* (Rev. 19:11-21) All the Bible testifies of His glorious return. The angels foretold it when they said, *Men of Galilee, why do you stand gazing up into heaven? This same Jesus, who was taken up from you into heaven, will so come in like manner as you saw Him go into heaven.* (Acts 1:11) The apostles spoke of this tremendous event at the Lord's supper when they said, *For as often as you eat this bread and drink this cup, you proclaim the Lord's death till He comes.* (1 Cor. 11:26) Our Lord Himself said, *In My Father's house are many mansions; if it were not so, I would have told you. I go to prepare a place for you, and if I go and prepare a place for you, I will come again and receive you to Myself; that where I am, there you may be also.* (John 14:2-3) What is this falling stone upon the statue of Nebuchadnezzar's dream? It is, without doubt, the second coming of Christ. Our Lord is coming back to rule over the earth as King of kings and Lord of lords. The knowledge of this fact gives us much hope and encouragement as we seek to address the culture of our day.

We now come to the "where" question. Where does the stone strike the statute? This is vitally important. It does not strike the statue in the head. Our Lord did not return to rule and reign during the days of the Babylonian Empire. One might think he would strike the head to bring the statue down but not true. The stone does not strike the statue in the chest. One might think the area of the heart would be most vulnerable but no, he did not return during the Medeo-Persian Empire. Someone else might think the stone would strike the statue in the abdomen. After all, that is where the vital organs exist. But he did not come to reign and rule during the days of the Greek Empire. Someone else might think the best place to bring down the statue would be in the legs. Anyone who has played football has known the fundamentals of tackling involve taking the legs out from under the runner. But our Lord did not establish His kingdom during the days of the Roman Empire. Note carefully that the stone strikes the statue in the feet (Daniel 2:34). The last form of Gentile world power will be in existence when the stone crushes human history. We seem to be living in these very prophetic days. Note that when the stone strikes the feet the whole structure comes tumbling down (Daniel 2:35). When our Lord Jesus Christ returns, human history and the governments of this world will come to an end. Daniel 2:35 reveals that nothing will remain but the dust and it will be blown away by the wind.

We come now to the "when" question. When will this all take place? It will take place when all the great world powers have passed away and the remnant of the last one emerges into a multi-nation confederacy. That may well be happening at this writing. The Eurodollar could be an expression of this confederacy. There will never be another world empire according to the Bible. Time and time again it appeared that this prophecy might fail. It looked as though Napoleon Bonaparte would conquer the world and Daniel's prophesy would fail. But Napoleon met his own Waterloo and the emperor died alone as a refugee on the rocky isle of Helena. Why? Because God said 2,600 years ago that the last world empire would be the iron legs of Rome. Hitler made some incredible statements about world dominion but perished with them in the flames of Germany. When I was a school boy Nikita Khrushchev of Russia said that the Soviet Union would never have to defeat America because she would simply crumble in her own hands, and I have lived to see his own empire crumble. Why? Because God said over two and a half millennia ago that the last world empire would be the iron legs of Rome.

What do we see here? The empire does not strike back, the empire strikes out! All world empires are temporary. One comes after another and they do not strike back, they all strike out. As we confront our culture with Daniel we're reminded of the futility of putting faith in human governments. We see our only hope in a stone that is not cut with human hands. The Lord Jesus Christ is coming to fill the earth with a kingdom of peace and glory. When will these things come to pass? They come to pass when the toes of Daniel emerge in human history.

Next we come to the "how" question. How will this statue fall? The stone strikes it with destructive force. It shatters. It breaks. It crushes (Dan. 2:34-35). This is not the meek and mild and lowly Jesus on the back of a donkey. This is King Jesus coming to reign and rule. In his own apocalyptic discourse on the Mount of Olives Jesus says, *At that time the sign of the Son of Man will appear in the sky, and all the nations of the earth will mourn. They will see the Son of Man coming on the clouds of the sky, with power and great glory.* (Matt. 24:30) The kingdoms of this world will be crushed by sudden events. The world may be saying "peace, peace," when all of a sudden destruction smites the whole system. The action of this stone is nothing short of the judgment of God upon this world system.

Finally, we come to the "why" question. God has a purpose. He is destroying the old. Why? To bring in the new. John on Patmos said, *Then I saw a new heaven and a new earth, for the first heaven and the first earth had passed away, and there was no longer any sea. I saw the Holy City, the new Jerusalem, coming down out of heaven from God, prepared as a bride beautifully dressed for her husband.* (Rev. 21:1-2) God is going to cleanse and purge this planet before this event. He is going to set up His kingdom and then usher in eternity. This is a picture of the stone growing throughout the whole world. Our Lord Jesus is coming into our war-weary and terrorist-tormented world during the time of the ten toes of Daniel 2 to right our world and end the *times of the Gentiles*.

Daniel tells us that the *rock that struck the statue became a huge mountain*. (Dan. 2:35) Here is the kingdom of God filling the earth. Here is the great millennial reign of Christ. In that day, men shall *beat your plowshares into swords and your pruning hooks into spears*. (Joel 3:10) John reminds us that *the kingdoms of this world have become the kingdoms of our Lord and of His Christ, and He shall reign forever and ever.* (Rev. 11:15) This is also the time described by King David in Psalm 72:11 when he says, *Yes, all kings shall fall down before Him; All nations shall serve Him.* This is the event Paul spoke of in the Philippian letter when he said *that at the name of Jesus every knee should bow, of those in heaven, and of those on earth, and of those under the earth, and that every tongue should confess that Jesus Christ is Lord, to the glory of God the Father.* (Phil. 2:10-11) This is what we are praying when we pray the model prayer and request, *Your kingdom come, Your will be done on earth as it is in heaven.* (Luke 11:2) Do you see it? No wonder John closed the Apocalypse with a prayer — "Even so come Lord Jesus."

Can you see it? The Gentile rule of the earth is destroying itself and disintegrating. The Jews have gathered back in the land. The props are in place. It was this second coming of Christ that Isaac Watts had in mind rather than the first coming of Christ when he wrote, "Joy to the world! the Lord is come; Let earth receive her King." He went on to say, "He rules the world with truth and grace, and makes the nations prove the glories of His righteousness and wonders of His love."

The end is approaching. The next great event in human history is the coming of our Lord. This stone, the Lord Jesus Christ, is returning to smite the nations and set up His kingdom. In the words of Daniel, *It shall break in pieces and consume all these kingdoms and it shall stand forever.* (Dan. 2:44) He also reminds us that this dream is certain and this interpretation is sure.

Note the outcome. Daniel 2:46-49 unfolds with Daniel becoming the virtual prime minister of Babylon through the interpretation of this dream. He brought his three friends into places of leadership. He did not forget his prayer partners and friends. Note the reaction of Nebuchadnezzar. *Truly your God is the God of gods, the Lord of kings and a revealer of secrets.* (Dan. 2:47) How sad it is that Nebuchadnezzar did not confess, "Your God is my God." David did not say, "The Lord is **a** shepherd." He said, *The Lord is MY shepherd.* Thomas did not say, "**a** Lord and **a** God." Thomas exclaimed, ***My** Lord and **my** God.* But Nebuchadnezzar could only say, *Your God is **a** god.* Things are not a whole lot different today. To many people he is just another god. He is some unknown force in everything and everyone. Even among some churches our Lord has lost His exclusivity. Can you say, "Your God is my God?"

This truth should be a great encouragement to us as we seek to live in the midst of the pagan culture that is all around us. God reveals to us the scope of human history with a statue. We don't have to wonder. We can be sure. He also reveals the hope of human history with a stone. Are you putting your hope in a losing cause by committing yourself to this present world and its own systems? The kingdoms of this world are only temporary. Babylon was a city of gold but it never rose again. Our faith should be placed in the coming Lord Jesus and His kingdom. Unlike the Babylonian Empire, He does not strike out. He is coming to strike back. The Babylonian Empire died. Our Lord died but He rose again and is coming back to rule and reign.

Yes, my friend Byron Forrester watched the video of the Super Bowl several times but it had already happened. We have the video of the final Super Bowl of human history and the game has not even been played on the field as of yet. It takes the fear and the suspense out of life. While others around us are wringing their hands, stomping their feet, and not knowing what to do we have already seen how it is all going to end. This should give us tremendous confidence as we seek to engage our culture today.

Yes, *there is a God in heaven who reveals secrets.* (Dan. 2:28) If we truly believe this what are we going to do about it? God has given us the video. Look at it. Watch it. Study it. We're going to win. He is coming for us! Knowing how it is all going to end tomorrow should give us great confidence to keep going today in engaging our culture. Daniel is reminding us that God has not abdicated His throne. He is still in charge of human history and that means mine and yours! He is our only hope.

Part Three

You have what you tolerate

During my days of pastoring at the First Baptist Church in Dallas I had many wonderful visits with a very unique man who was in the midst of a life-threatening illness, which eventually ended in his death. He loved his Lord and hc lifted me up each time I was with him. His name was Jack Evans and he was a former mayor of the City of Dallas. Jack coined a saying that hangs on wall plaques in the offices of many business leaders of our city. His often-used quotc says, "You have what you tolerate."

When we think about that statement, "you have what you tolerate," we see that it is true in every area of our lives. Parents who tolerate their children talking back to them will eventually reap what they sow. I was fortunate to have had a mom and dad who did not tolerate disrespect and my wife and I did not tolerate it from our children either. Yes, you have what you tolerate. This statement is true if you're teaching in a classroom of students. I had professors who did not tolerate work that was less than our best. "You have what you tolerate" is true if you're coaching an athletic team. Coaches who tolerate sloppy practices have sloppy plays when it is game time. It is also true in church work. Those churches that tolerate mediocrity and are simply reactive instead of proactive lack productivity in the long haul. Yes, Jack Evans had it right — "You have what you tolerate!"

We are living in a world culture where the church has tolerated things for so long that these words have come home to roost. We have today what we tolerated yesterday. Tolerance seems to be the law of our land, and today it has a different meaning than it did a few years ago. Tolerance used to mean that in America we recognized and respected others' beliefs without sharing them. Today tolerance means that everyone's values, everyone's belief systems, everyone's lifestyles, are acceptable. Tolerance today says that all truth claims are equal. The one thing that many people fear today is simply being called intolerant. We have been so formed into the mold of our culture that we in the church now have what we tolerate.

Josh McDowell has spent a lifetime taking the Gospel to college campuses. Recently, Josh mentioned that he has always known heckling but a few years ago it took on a different form. Yesterday college students exclaimed, "Prove it; I don't believe that, prove the claims of Christ." Today, however, they exclaim, "What right have you to say that? You're intolerant, you're a bigot!" John 3:16 has been replaced today with Matthew 7:1, *Judge not that you be not judged.* Tolerance is more important than truth in many circles.

There are a myriad of news shows with interview formats on television today. CNN has their *Crossfire* or *Larry King Live*. Fox News has many programs that are growing rapidly in popularity. While watching one such show recently I wondered what would happen if the Lord Jesus Christ were being interviewed on one of those programs today. What would happen if He were taking calls as people do on modern news talk shows? If He was on one of those programs and said what He said in the Gospels, He would be ridiculed. He would be called intolerant and even referred to as a bigot. For example, take what He said to the woman at the well in John 4. The Lord Jesus spoke to her about her lifestyle and said, *Go, call your husband and come here*. When she replied that she didn't have one He reiterated, *You have well said, "I have no husband," for you have had five husbands, and the one whom you now have is not your husband*. (John 4:18) Can you see Him saying that to someone who called in on *Larry King Live?* They would be quick to say, "Who do you think you are? You're intolerant! You're a bigot." Or, what if He were to say to our modern world in a forum like that today, "You do not know what you worship, but we do, we worship God in spirit and truth." Why, they would turn on Him and exclaim, "What right do you have to say that?" Why? Because tolerance is the theme of our day. That is, everyone's values, beliefs, lifestyles and truth claims are equal in the eyes of our modern culture.

Tolerance is the only absolute of today's culture. From every avenue we are being taught to be tolerant of alternative lifestyles. We often hear men and women quote our Lord today by saying, *Neither do I condemn you.* (John 8:11). If you remember, the context is with the woman taken in adultery, in the very act of sexual sin. However, few people today want to say all that Jesus said and quote the last part of the verse, *Go and sin no more.* Here we find the present tense and the imperative mood. This is not a suggestion. Our Lord Jesus said go and stop sinning! Yes, He did not condemn her but He also said *go and stop your sinning.* The Lord Jesus took the woman where she was but she didn't stay there. It is true the woman was a harlot but not after she met our Lord. Paul says in I Cor. 6:11, *And such were some of you.* He goes on to say, *But you were washed.* He identifies homosexuals and adulterers and thieves in the church at Corinth but he reveals that they did not stay that way. Do you think those drunkards stayed in the choir at Corinth? No, even though they were drunkards in the past they began to *sin no more.* The church did not tolerate that alternative lifestyle. Do you think that thieves continued to take up the offering? Can you hear someone saying, "Watch your purse, Bob is taking the offering today!" No, the church did not tolerate alternative lifestyles. What about the homosexual or the adulterer? Do you know what happened? Their lives were changed. They were transformed by the power of God.

We live in a world that teaches our kids tolerance at almost every hand. It is telling them in a myriad of ways that everyone's values, everyone's belief systems, everyone's lifestyles, and everyone's truth claims are equal. In fact, we're instilling in the minds of our young adults that there are no moral absolutes, no absolute truth. We're seeing this growing more and more even in the church. Some churches sponsor prayer meetings with Christians and Jews and Muslims and other religions all praying to the "same God." All faiths are equal in the eyes of many. We may call it harmony but it is spelled "T-O-L-E-R-A-N-C-E." How tolerant do you think our Jewish friends are when they feel efforts of evangelism are directed at them and are a means to destroy their own belief system? They're not very tolerant. How tolerant do you think our Muslim friends would be in a culture that spoke about Mohammed like the American culture is speaking about the Lord Jesus today? Recently the government sponsored an art show in New York City with a crucifix in a bottle of urine. Yes, we have today what we tolerated yesterday. And we will have tomorrow what we tolerate today.

We are living in an anti-Christian culture that continues to tolerate social ills that are contrary to the Word of God. We've been doing this for years. Why? Jack Evans said it best, "You have what you tolerate!"

From time to time there have been those who have stood up in the face of tolerance of their day. There's no more thrilling narrative in all of literature than the story of the deliverance of the three Hebrew young men from the burning fiery furnace. Is there anyone reading these words who finds themselves in a tight spot? Does anyone feel that there simply is no way out of your circumstances or situation? Then this chapter is for you. Shadrach, Meshach, and Abednego's victory is a comfort and a challenge to us today in the midst of a tolerant world. It is the story of faith triumphing over fear. It is the story of courage triumphing over cowardice. It is the story of conviction triumphing over compromise. It is the story of three young men who did not bow to the god of tolerance. Perhaps some of you, like them, have done what is right. You took your own stand. And still you found yourself in your own fiery furnace. The third chapter of Daniel has to do with what happens to us when we are obedient to the Word of God, when we do what is right, and still end up in a fiery furnace of life.

In this chapter we learn many things. God never promises to keep us out of the fiery furnace. He did not keep Shadrach, Meshach, and Abednego out. However, He got in with them. And, He will get in with you. And you, like them, can come out stronger. Our God is the same God who loosed their bonds and walked with them in the midst of the flames.

In a world screaming for tolerance our lives will be tested. The decisions you make this week will be governed by one of two things, either inner principle or outer pressure. That is, either by the Word of God or by the world's system. If you allow God's word to dictate your inner principle then you will react to life's fiery furnaces with faith and the result will be deliverance. If you allow the world to dictate your outer pressures then you will react with fear and the result will be bondage. Shadrach, Meshach, and Abednego lived by inner principle. They got it from the Word of God. Others lived by outer pressure and they had what they tolerated.

In this volume we are seeking to learn how to stand in a culture that's increasingly pagan and anti-God. Daniel has been saying don't give in, don't give up, don't give out. Now, his three friends have something to say to us. They are saying to you and to me that in the face of a culture that is advocating tolerance at all costs, we must learn to live with pressure. We must learn to live with principle. We must learn to live with perspective. We must learn to live with protection. Jack Evans' words have never been more true — "You have what you tolerate!"

Chapter 6

Learning to live with pressure

Dan. 3:1-12

Our faith will be tested. King Nebuchadnezzar let his dream in Chapter 2 go to his head. He ended up building a great image of himself out on the plain of Dura. It was made of gold and stood 90 feet high. Placed out on the plain, it could be seen for miles as its golden image, nine stories tall, stood glistening in the sun. It must have been an awesome sight. Nebuchadnezzar called people from all around to the dedication service of his golden image. Daniel's account reveals that thousands of people gathered on the plain of Dura. The dedication program was planned out to the "n^{th} degree." As the orchestra began to play, all of the people were to bow down and worship the image of Nebuchadnezzar. Those who would not do so would meet a horrible fate. They would be thrown into Babylon's burning, fiery furnace. It was at this very point that the faith of these three young Hebrew men — Shadrach, Meshach, and Abednego — met their greatest test. Should they go along with the crowd, just this one time? After all, they could get lost in this great multitude of people and bow down along with them and hardly anyone would notice. Or should they stand out like a sore thumb, remain faithful to their convictions, and not bow down to the golden image? The test of faith eventually finds its way to all of us in some way.

In our current culture our own faith is being tested on every front. This has always been true for people who have followed after Christ. For John, the test of faith came on the rocky island of Patmos. For Paul, it was what he referred to as a thorn in the flesh. A fiery furnace for some of us might be some difficult circumstance or situation. It might be the loss of a job, a child on drugs, or any number of other challenges that might come our way in our contemporary culture. Our faith will be tested. There's a sense in which we live out there on the plain of Dura ourselves every week. Our world is calling for tolerance all around us. It is calling us to join the others in bowing down to other gods. In the face of a culture that is advocating tolerance we must learn to live with outside pressures. They are not going to go away.

The first 12 verses of the third chapter of Daniel paint a very intriguing picture. They are woven throughout with what we would call today "peer pressure." All the nations of the region were subject to Babylon. Everyone had sent delegates to this great event. The city was decorated to perfection. This was the biggest day in the history of Babylon.

There, standing almost nine stories tall and shining in the morning sun, was the great image of Nebuchadnezzar. The word came. The orchestra began to play. Everyone across the plain of Dura began to bow down to worship the image. After all, if they refused they would be thrown into the burning, fiery furnace.

It is interesting to note who was there. The Bible refers to *the satraps, the administrators, the governors, the counselors, the treasurers, the judges, the magistrates, and all the officials of the provinces...* (Dan. 3:2) In other words, all the big shots had gathered. Like a bunch of rubber stamps with no character and no integrity, they all bowed down to the image, surrendering to the peer pressure at hand. After all, they must have thought, "We have to keep our jobs." There are a lot of young people in our contemporary culture out on the plain of Dura today. They have bought into the philosophy that tells them they will not be popular unless they go along with the crowd, unless they bow down with the others. After all, they're convinced that everyone else is doing it so why not go ahead and bow down. There are a lot of men and women in the business world today trying to get ahead out there on the plain of Dura. Peer pressure is prevalent in our contemporary culture.

Shadrach, Meshach, and Abednego could have rationalized and reasoned like a lot of men and women do today. They could have said, "Nebuchadnezzar has treated us pretty well all these years. He has appointed us to positions of honor. He has empowered us with a good education and a good job. If we don't bow down we'll look pretty unappreciative. After all, we're here in Babylon now and when in Babylon we should do as the Babylonians do. Anyway, the end justifies the means. It's all situational anyway." But if you read the text you will notice that there's not a hint of this type of attitude anywhere in their minds. These three young men never entertained one of those thoughts. They had already decided which way they were going to turn before they reached this intersection in life.

There was a tremendous amount of pressure on these young Hebrews to conform. "Go ahead," others told them, "get out there on the plain with them. There are thousands of others out there." And then it happened. The band began to play and everyone bowed down. Everyone out there on the plain of Dura bowed down…except three young men. They stood out like three sore thumbs that day on the plain of Dura. When the music starts and we feel our own peer pressure, we will do one of two things. If we're controlled by the Word we will respond with conviction. If we're controlled by the world we will respond with compromise. On the plain of Dura this week we will find ourselves in one of these two groups. Look at all those people out there on the plain of Dura. They did not know how to live with pressure. Peer pressure said to bow down so they all compromised. But three young men stood up! How could they? Their lives were governed by inner principle and not outer pressure. They had learned how to live with pressure. Too many of us are not engaging our culture today because we have not learned this lesson. We have bought in to the peer pressure of the pluralism of our day and we have what we tolerate.

Shadrach, Meshach, and Abednego could have said, "I'm bowing down on the outside but I'm standing up on the inside." Had some of us in the church today been out there on the plain of Dura that day we might have been prone to say, "We can't fight the system. We might as well go along. After all, God knows how we really feel. We do not want to offend Nebuchadnezzar because we would like to win him to our faith. We will be of no use to God if we're dead in a fiery furnace so let's go ahead and bow down just this one time for now." This happens on the plain of Dura every day with men and women who are called by the name of Christ. Compromise has taken the place of conviction in the vocabularies of many followers of Christ. In fact, the very word "conviction" seems to be a lost word in the Christian vocabulary.

Some of us will never engage our culture as long as we continue to bow to peer pressure. This may be the greatest test of faith today. Nebuchadnezzar's golden image was nothing more than an attempt to substitute man-worship for God-worship. It is easy to go along with the crowd. It is difficult to be in the minority. We have a lot of opinions in the church today, but do not seem to have as many convictions. Opinion is based on what we think. Conviction is based upon what God says!

Idols are not confined to the plain of Dura. We bow down before all kinds of idols in our contemporary culture. Some of us make idols of possessions or people or our own popularity, or any number of projects. Pleasure is the god of many. A lot of us know what the Scripture says but we still bow down when peer pressure comes our way. Why? Could it be because what others think is more important to us than what God says? Let me repeat that in a more personal way. Is what others think more important to you than what God says? Why should we think that in our day Christians can live free from these outer pressures to bow down? The real tragedy is that many are so spiritually desensitized they're not even aware of the pressures any more. Many simply just bow down on their own plain of Dura without any thought about it whatsoever.

Perhaps the hymn writer asked the question best. "Must I be carried to the skies on flow'ry beds of ease, while others fought to win the prize, and sailed thro' bloody seas? Sure I must fight if I would reign; Increase my courage, Lord! I'll bear the toil, endure the pain, supported by Thy Word." The truth is we need each other. There's a real dynamic at play here. If your name is Shadrach you need a Meshach and Abednego to stand with you. These three friends found strength not only in their God but also with each other. As we attempt to address and engage our contemporary culture there's a dynamic involved in standing with one another.

When the Lord Jesus Christ is ruling our life we respond out on the plain of Dura with conviction. In the face of a world that's advocating tolerance at all cost we must learn to live with pressure. Our faith will be tested. Out there tomorrow on our own plain where tolerance is the byword and everyone is bowing down, we, too, will hear the music begin to play. Remember, you have what you tolerate! In the face of a culture advocating tolerance at all cost we must learn to live with pressure. What God says is so much more important than what we might think or others might say.

Chapter 7

Learning to live with principle

Dan. 3:13-16

Much of our pluralistic American culture points to those of us who are evangelical Christians as being the single greatest intolerant force in America. In a myriad of subtle ways this continues to be branded into the American psyche. However, in reality it is our culture and its world system that is intolerant to Christians who believe that the Word of God is infallible, trustworthy, and true. This is nothing new. It has always been this way. Tolerance is the theme in America today. Americans are taught to tolerate everyone except those of us who believe in absolute truth. These advocates of tolerance have a favorite verse. It is Matt. 7:1; *Judge not, that you be not judged.* Unfortunately, they take it out of context for if we read verse 2 we see that our Lord is speaking about self-righteousness, setting ourselves up to judge others who have a speck in their eye when we have a beam in our own eye and are blinded to our own sin.

If learning to live with pressure has to do with peer pressure, then learning to live with principle has to do with fear pressure. After hearing that these three Hebrew young men would not bow to his golden image, Nebuchadnezzar in a rage of fury called Shadrach, Meshach, and Abednego into his presence. He cannot believe what he has heard. The audacity of these three young men not bowing before his image! So that there might be no misunderstanding he gives them another opportunity. They can bow or they can burn. This is no longer peer pressure. Now fear pressure comes into play.

When fear pressure comes our way we will do one of two things. If we're controlled by the Word we will respond with courage. However, if we are controlled by the world and its friendship then we will respond with cowardice. Listen to the response of these three faithful men; *...our God whom we serve is able to deliver us from the burning fiery furnace, and He will deliver us from your hand, O king. But if not, let it be known to you, O king, that we do not serve your gods, nor will we worship the gold image which you have set up*. (Dan. 3:17-18) They responded with courage because their lives were governed by the Word of God and they drew the line at the Word of God. Remember, Shadrach, Meshach, and Abednego were not their real names. Their real names were Hananiah, Mishael, and Azariah. But, they tolerated their name change because there was no clear biblical admonition regarding it. They did the same with the language and the same with the literature. But like their friend Daniel, they drew the line when it came to the Word of God. Shadrach, Meshach, and Abednego knew that Exodus 20:3-4 carried with it the admonition from God Himself that *you shall have no other gods before Me. You shall not make for yourself a carved image — any likeness of anything that is in heaven above, or that is in the earth beneath, or that is in the water under the earth.* This command was explicit to these Hebrew young men. They also had Deuteronomy 8: 2 burning in their heart. Moses had said, *And you shall remember that the Lord your God led you all the way these forty years in the wilderness, to humble you and test you, to know what was in your heart, whether you would keep His commandments or not.* They knew God was testing them. Our faith will be tested. If the devil cannot get us to bow to peer pressure he will seek to get us to bend to fear pressure.

Fear pressure is where we find the real pressure to conform. There is the fear of losing our job if we do not bow. There's the fear of being different. Some times we're so convinced that everyone else is bowing. There is so much pressure to go along with our contemporary culture. How many young men and women have lost their virginity because of fear pressure? They were simply afraid to be different, afraid they may not be popular. They were convinced that everyone was bowing down. In the face of outer pressure these three young men were governed by inner principle and they stood tall! This is character. Character is functioning with inner principle and not yielding to outer pressure. They let Nebuchadnezzar know that right was right and wrong was wrong and some things are non-negotiable. It is a tragic thing that many who would never think of bowing to peer pressure on the plain of Dura bend to fear pressure when getting before the king.

Nebuchadnezzar looked them in the eye and asked, *is it true?* (Dan. 3:14) That is a good question. It is a question all of us ought to be asking ourselves. Is it true? This is really the question the world seems to be asking today. The world sees so many of us in church on Sundays and then bowing down on the plain of Dura on Monday. The world, like Nebuchadnezzar, wants to know, "Is it true?" Or, is it just something we say we believe but when we get out on the plain of Dura we're really no different from all the rest. Is it true?

These verses bring us face to face with the issue of civil disobedience. What is a Christian to do when the king makes a decree with which we do not agree? What about the issue of civil disobedience? Can we learn anything from Shadrach, Meshach, and Abednego at this point? After all, did not our Lord himself say that we were to be subject to the authorities that are over us? And, here are these three men refusing to do what the government told them to do. When is it okay to disobey the civil authority? Where do we draw the line? Romans 13:1 says, *Let every soul be subject to the governing authorities*. The Bible tells us that it is "appointed by God." Peter tells us *therefore submit yourselves to every ordinance of man for the Lord's sake, whether to the king as supreme, or to governors.* (I Peter. 2:13-14) However, there are times in Scripture that we have to disobey civil law in order to obey God's law. The first chapter of Exodus is one such experience.

The Hebrew midwives disobeyed the civil law of destroying all the male Hebrew children by delivering and protecting them. We also see it in Daniel 3 with Nebuchadnezzar's golden image on the plain of Dura. In the New Testament we find it in the fourth and fifth chapters of Acts. We hear the early apostles saying, "We ought to obey God rather than men." Note that in all these cases a common thread is apparent. There is a direct specific conflict between man's law and God's law. And, note also, that believers are willing to pay the price for their consequences of civil disobedience. We have a biblical responsibility to submit and support governmental authority. All authority comes from God. The Bible reminds us that governmental authorities are "God's ministers." Observance of the law is a positive public testimony of our faith. It is the right thing to do. The only biblical exceptions are those that are outlined above.

In the face of the world that's advocating tolerance at all cost we must learn to live with inner principle. There will be those this week that will try to get us to bow on the plain of Dura and we must learn to live within our principle. We must draw the line with the Word of God. Like Daniel, like Shadrach, Meshach, and Abednego, we must let the word so dwell in us that we live with conviction and not with compromise. In the face of a world that advocates tolerance at all cost we must learn to live not only with pressure but also with principle.

Chapter 8

Learning to live with perspective

Dan. 3:17-18

Tolerance was as much the byword in ancient Babylon as it is in modern America. Everyone had bowed down to worship Nebuchadnezzar's golden image except the three Hebrew young men. When faced with Nebuchadnezzar's challenge to provide an answer for their behavior they replied, *if that is the case, our God whom we serve is able to deliver us from the burning fiery furnace, and he will deliver us from your hand, O king. But if not, let it be known to you, O king, that we do not serve your gods nor will we worship the golden image which you have set up*. (Dan. 3:17-18) Theirs' was an immediate reply. They did not even have to think about it.

Listen to their response. "Our God." Do you sense the camaraderie here? They were going through this together. They were standing together not only out there on the plain of Dura but also before the king and eventually in the fiery furnace. The truth is, we need each other as we seek victory and raise our children in a pagan culture. We, too, need to learn to live with perspective. He is "our God."

They went on to say, "Whom we serve." Some of us may be able to say "our God" but can we complete the phrase with "whom we serve?" We sometimes wonder why we succumb so easily to peer pressure or fear pressure. It is our God *whom we serve* that is able to deliver us. As a pastor for many years I watched men and women who professed Christ but did not do much in serving Him. When the crisis hour came they so often faced it with cowardice because they bowed down on the plain of Dura. On the other hand, I've watched those who serve the Lord Jesus Christ faithfully come to the crisis of the testing of their faith and they did so with courage, because in service to Him their lives were geared by the Word of God. Learning to live with perspective is not simply something we say but something we do.

These young men also remind us that *our God whom we serve is able to deliver us*. This is not superficial speculation but solid conviction based on the Word of God. Here were three young men who knew the Word of God and staked their lives on it by faith and believed that their God was able. This is really the issue isn't it? God is able. It is when we settle this in our mind and learn to live with this type of perspective that we really have no problem out there on our own plain of Dura.

Whatever our need, He is able. Do we need grace? *And* ***God is able*** *to make all grace abound toward you,* (2 Cor. 9:8). Do we need to overcome temptation? *For in that He Himself has suffered, being tempted,* ***He is able*** *to aid those who are tempted.* (Heb. 2:18) Do we need salvation? *Therefore* ***He is also able*** *to save to the uttermost those who come to God through Him...* (Heb. 7:25) Do we need security? Paul said *...I know whom I have believed and am persuaded that* ***He is able*** *to keep what I have committed to Him until that Day.* (2 Tim. 1:12) Do we need strength? *Now to* ***Him who is able*** *to keep you from stumbling, And to present you faultless before the presence of His glory with exceeding joy...* (Jude 1:24) If we're not sure that our God is able then we may not be able to say "our God" at all, much less *whom we serve.*

The real secret to their perspective is found in Daniel 3:18. *But if not, let it be known to you, O king, that we do not serve your gods, nor will we worship the gold image which you have set up.* Their faith was not based on God's performance. Their faith was based upon the Lord alone. A lot of men and women have faith as long as they have blessings or feelings or some other trinket. Shadrach, Meshach, and Abednego's faith was in the living God. It was not in what they could get from Him. Sometimes we must say this in the face of our final enemy, death. Yes, He is able to deliver us "but if not" we still will not bow down. Sometimes we have to say this in the face of sickness. He is able to deliver us *but if not...* Sometimes we have to say this in the face of business failure.

He is able to deliver us…*but if not*… We have to say it in times of frustration or times of defeat. He is able to deliver us…*but if not*… Sometimes when we pray and seemingly receive no answer we say it again. He is able to deliver us…*but if not*… The issue is never God's ability. He is able! The issue is wrapped in His sovereign will.

Some people have the idea that if they are delivered from a fiery furnace of life that everyone should join in the celebration, "but if not" we should quietly hide so as not to damage God's reputation nor show any of our own lack of faith. What kind of God is this? This is the very reason some television healers screen their people before they let them on the stage. A recent cable news program interviewed a mother of a paraplegic boy who came to just such a "miracle service" hours early. She and her son were taken to another room and never even got into the auditorium. Such incidents are not only tragedies, but are travesties to the Gospel.

We're reminded that the same God that gave to Job also was the same God that took from Job. The same God who delivered Simon Peter from prison allowed James to be martyred by the sword in the same chapter in Acts. The same God that allowed John the Baptist's head to be chopped off is the same God that delivered others in other circumstances and situations. The perspective, "but if not," is closely akin to what Job said, *even though he slay me yet I will trust him.* (Job 13-15) It's also close to Esther's classic pronouncement, *If I perish, I perish.* (Est. 4:16)

When these three young men say, *but if not,* they are demonstrating a level of mature faith. Look at them. Unlike some today who demand of God and tell Him what he has to do, they were not instructing God. They were abandoning themselves to Him much like our Lord did in Gethsemane Garden. I've always wondered where some people get off dictating to God what He has or has not to do, demanding Him to do this or demanding Him to do that. Our God is sovereign which simply means He always does what he pleases and is always pleased with what He does. These folks who do not live with the *but if not* perspective of life and continue to demand and claim things from God are seldom found in the hospitals holding the hand of some sweet lady with cancer who is full of faith herself. Our Lord Jesus took his healing ministry into the marketplace. He went to people where they were at such places as the Pool of Bethesda. He did not go to Jerusalem, rent the amphitheater, and announce a big meeting for those who could physically get there and then go through a screening process to see who would be allowed on stage. Yes, he is able to deliver us from the burning fiery furnace…*but if not*…we still will not bow down.

Whether God delivers us from the furnace or not does not change our conviction that "He is able." If one claims to have lost their faith because of a situation where God did not come through like they thought He should, then it is proof that their faith was only in performance. We all know of people who have quit the race because they said our God whom we serve is able, but they never learned to complete the sentence…*but if not*…

It is interesting to me that Shadrach, Meshach, and Abednego did not even ask God to deliver them. They simply threw themselves upon Him and His sovereign will for their lives and come what may they were going to praise His wonderful name. There are a lot of people today who want to stand tall in the day of faith's victory but few who really know how to stand tall in the day of faith's tests and trials. Everyone wants to walk across the stage and receive their diploma but not everyone wants to pay the price of hard study and term papers and multiple tests.

Shadrach, Meshach, and Abednego would not bow to peer pressure and they would not bend to fear pressure. Their battle was won right here at this very place. It wasn't won in the fiery furnace, it was won when they came to live not only with pressure and principle but also with perspective. We should never wait until we get into a fiery furnace to try and decide what to do. These three young men did not burn because they did not bow nor bend. Some of us burn in the fiery furnace because, before we ever get there, we bow to peer pressure or bend to fear pressure. Why? Because we make too many of our decisions based on outer pressure instead of inner principle. And thus, we find our lives filled with compromise and cowardice instead of conviction and courage as we face our contemporary culture.

In the face of a world that advocates tolerance at all cost we must learn to live with pressure. We must learn to live with principle. And, above all, we need to learn to live with perspective. Our God whom we serve is able...*but if not!*

Chapter 9

Learning to live with protection

Dan. 3:19-30

Now we find our three young friends *bound…and cast into the midst of the burning fiery furnace*. (Dan. 3:21) They could not get out now if they tried. They were bound in the midst of the fiery furnace. There was nowhere to go. Have we ever felt like that in our own culture that surrounds us? Some of us need to learn to live with His protection. A careful reading of the text will reveal that the fiery furnace is there for two very good reasons: our good and His glory.

Note that one of the byproducts of the three Hebrew young men being in the fiery furnace was that it turned out for their own good. All they had in the fiery furnace was the promise of God. They were standing on Isaiah 43:2, *When you walk through the fire, you shall not be burned, nor shall the flame scorch you.* I believe had the hymn been written they would have been singing, "When thro' fiery trials thy pathway shall lie, My grace, all sufficient, shall be thy supply; the flame shall not hurt thee; I only design thy dross to consume, and thy gold to refine." God could have delivered them from the fiery furnace but He had a better plan. And, His plan ultimately worked for their good and His own glory. Thus, He could have kept them from the fiery furnace. After all, He delivered all of Israel when He parted the Red Sea. He delivered them from starvation in the wilderness by providing manna every day from heaven. Yes, He is able to deliver us. However, God knew that deliverance "from" the fiery furnace was not nearly as significant as deliverance "in" the fiery furnace. It might be that some of us have missed God's purpose and plan for us because we got mad at Him when He didn't deliver us from our own fiery furnace. He hasn't forgotten us. Perhaps it is for our own good that His plan is to deliver you "in" your own fiery furnace.

Why should we think that we are immune to the trials of life? The Lord Jesus said our Father in heaven *sends rain on the just and on the unjust.* (Matt. 5:45) Ask Paul if he was immune to the trials of life. He was stoned at Lystra and left for dead. He spoke of a thorn in the flesh that continued to bother him. Ask Simon Peter if he was immune to the trials of life. He met his martyr's death by being crucified upside down. Ask the roll call of the faithful that are listed for us in the 11th chapter of Hebrews if they were immune to the trials of life. These were all people who learned to live with God's protection and made up their minds about the *but if nots* of life.

None of us are immune to the fiery furnace experiences of life. They often find their way to us for a variety of reasons. Some trials are for punishment. David found this out. He was told *the sword shall never depart from your house, because you have despised Me…* (II Sam. 12:10) Some trials are for prevention. Paul said, *And lest I should be exalted above measure by the abundance of the revelations, a thorn in the flesh was given to me…* (II Cor. 12:7) Some trials are for proof. Job said, *I have heard of You by the hearing of the ear, but now my eye sees You.* (Job 42:5) Some trials are for partnership. John, the Revelator, referred to himself as our *brother and companion in the tribulation* when he was on the isle of Patmos. (Rev. 1:9) Other trials are for profit. The writer of Hebrews relates that *indeed for a few days chastened us as seemed best to them, but He for our profit, that we may be partakers of His holiness.* (Heb. 12:10)

Look at Shadrach, Meshach, and Abednego in the fiery furnace. What happens when we do not bow nor bend? We do not burn! When Nebuchadnezzar looked into the furnace he exclaimed, *Look!…I see four men loose, walking in the midst of the fire; and they are not hurt, and the form of the fourth is like the Son of God.* (Dan. 3:25) Let's take a brief math lesson. How many went into the fiery furnace? Three. How many did Nebuchadnezzar see when he looked into the furnace? Four. How many came out? Three. Thus, we find that our Lord is still there. And if any of us are in the fiery furnace today and we look around, we'll find Him. Here lies an important lesson for each of us. When we walk through the fire it is helpful to have some faithful friends with us as well as the Lord himself. We do not have to go it alone.

Yes, the fiery furnace experiences of life could work out for our own good. The Bible says that their bonds were *loosed*. (Dan. 3:25) The only thing the fire burned away was that which bound them up. So often the flames of our own trials and testing sets us freer than we've ever been before. I've seen this happen. I've known men that were bound up with ropes of pride who went through a fiery furnace and came out free. The fiery furnace is for our good. Just look at Shadrach, Meshach, and Abednego!

Not only did they find freedom there in the fiery furnace but they also found fellowship. Nebuchadnezzar says there were four men walking around the furnace and the fourth was *like the son of God*. The Lord himself left His throne of glory and came down to walk through the fire with these three Hebrew young men who had taken a stand for Him. And, He will do the same for you. Don't quit in the time of testing. If you'll look around you'll find that you're not alone. God never promised to keep us out of the fiery furnace but He did say He would get in with us and when we come out on the other side it would be for our own good. Time and time again I've seen the Lord become so real to so many who've had fiery furnace experiences of life who have emerged with their bonds loosed never to be the same again.

These three young men believed in the promises of God. Their trust was in Him and they were a testimony to the king.

The result was that Nebuchadnezzar said, *Blessed be the God of Shadrach, Meshach, and Abednego who sent His angel and delivered his servants who trusted in Him.* (Dan. 3:28) Yes, in the face of a world that advocates tolerance on all sides and at all costs, they learned to live with pressure, principle, perspective, and protection.

Why does God allow the fiery furnace experiences of life? What is the purpose of this permissive will? Perhaps it is to fit us for higher service. Perhaps it is to separate the true believers from the pretenders. It's a lot easier to say, "I will not bow" until we're looking into the fiery furnace. God is watching. *For the eyes of the Lord run to and fro throughout the whole earth, to show Himself strong on behalf of those whose heart is loyal to Him.* (II Chron. 16:9) Yes, often the fiery furnace is for our own good.

The good news is that the fiery furnace experiences of life are not only for our own good but they ultimately serve for God's glory. Nebuchadnezzar said, *blessed be the God of Shadrach, Meshach, and Abednego who sent His angel and delivered His servants who trusted in Him…there is no other God who can deliver like this.* (Dan. 3:28-29) This is the very point that Simon Peter drove home in the New Testament when he says, *In this you greatly rejoice, though now for a little while, if need be, you have been grieved by various trials, that the genuineness of your faith, being much more precious than gold that perishes, though it is tested by fire, may be found to praise, honor, and glory at the revelation of Jesus Christ.* (I Peter 1:6-7)

King Nebuchadnezzar said, "There is no other god who can deliver like this." Then the king promoted Shadrach, Meshach, and Abednego in the province of Babylon. This is what the Gospel can do. The king who commanded the worshippers to bow down and worship his own image now bows himself before the King of all kings. He promoted these three young men. Yes, *When a man's ways please the Lord... He makes even his enemies to be at peace with him.* (Prov. 16:7) Men and women who honor God will not go unrewarded. Fiery furnaces of life are for our good and for God's glory. Yes, "when thro' fiery trials thy pathway shall lie, My grace, all sufficient, shall be thy supply; the flame shall not hurt thee; I only design thy dross to consume, and thy gold to refine."

Jack Evans had it right years ago. "You have what you tolerate!" We're living now in a world where tolerance has become the law of the land. We're told on every front that we should be tolerant in the sense that there is no absolute truth. "All religions are equal" is the constant cry. In the face of a world that advocates tolerance at all cost we must learn to live with pressure. Shadrach, Meshach, and Abednego did and so can we. We must learn to live with principle. These three young men had it and so can we. We must learn to live with perspective. They lived with the "but if not" attitude. So can we. We must learn to live with protection. The fiery furnace is for our good and His glory.

What do we learn out there on the plain of Dura and in the fiery furnace? We learn that God is in control. We learn that His finger is on the thermostat. And guess what? He still would have been in control had He allowed Shadrach, Meshach, and Abednego to perish in the flames. There are thousands of martyrs that have met that fate throughout church history. Yes, our God is able to deliver us…*but if not*…we still will not bow down.

We all go out there on the plain of Dura every week. Most of the people with whom we come in contact will be advocating tolerance. Most of them will go ahead and bow down — it's just a lot easier. Just like a bunch of rubber stamps with no character and no integrity, many people who are called by the name of Christ will do the same. Perhaps it will be because of peer pressure or perhaps because of fear pressure.

What will it be for you? Will your life be governed by inner principle…or outer pressure? You will have what you tolerate. There are two voices calling out to us today. One is the voice of tolerance and the other is the voice of truth. At a recent funeral I heard someone say, "All of us are going to the same place — some of us are simply taking different roads with different styles and different ways." That is the voice of tolerance. The voice of truth reveals the words of Christ, *I am the way, the truth, and the life. No one comes to the Father except through Me.* (John 14:6) The real question is which are you going to believe? Yes, you have what you tolerate!

Part Four

On a search for significance

There's an amazing transition taking place among the baby boomer generation in American culture today. It is a move from success to significance. This generation has acquired more possessions, more power, and more positions than any generation in human history. It set out to find success in life and found it. But guess what? This generation still has an emptiness inside. This generation also leads every generation in human history in such things as divorce, suicide, drug addition and loneliness.

Therefore, a significant segment of American culture is on a search today. It is a search for significance, fulfillment, a sense of purpose and authenticity. It is not a new search. By the world standards one of the most successful men in history made his transition from success to significance and recorded it here in the fourth chapter of Daniel for all prosperity. There are a lot of people in our culture on the same search today. The problem is that many still think significance is found in the successes of the worldly culture. Most men and women are still looking in all the wrong places. Some think that if they can do something better than anyone else they will find significance. So, they try to sell more policies, live in a bigger home, drive a fancier car, get their kids in better schools, and build bigger kingdoms.

Our culture is filled with the success syndrome. Most of the books we read are designed to make us the greatest. They tell us the way up is up! But in Daniel Chapter 4, King Nebuchadnezzar found the fallacy of this philosophy. In fact, he tells us that the way up is down!

Our culture says, "build up self-confidence." Our Bible says, *...put no confidence in the flesh...*(Phil. 3:3) Our culture says "promote yourself." Our Bible says we are to *crucify ourselves.* (Gal. 2:20) Our culture tells us "we must increase." Our Bible tells us that *He must increase, but I must decrease.* (John 3:30) Our culture tells us to "never be satisfied." Our Bible tells us that we are to learn *whatever state I am, to be content.* (Phil. 4:11) Our culture tells us to "put ourselves out front." Our Bible tells us we are to *deny ourselves.* (Luke 9:23) Our culture tells us, "you're number one!" Our Bible tells us we are to *humble ourselves under the mighty hand of God.* (I Peter 5:6)

What is your particular goal in life? Is it success...or significance? Do you want to be a successful parent or a significant parent? Do you want to be a successful member of society or a significant member of society? As we come to Daniel Chapter 4 we see one of the most successful men in all of world history. Nebuchadnezzar had achieved wealth, power, and everything else that goes with it. Daniel Chapter 4 is his own story. It is his own journey from success to significance. Nebuchadnezzar came to the conclusion that *the Most High rules in the kingdom of men…* (Dan. 4:17) This realization, *that the Most High rules over the affairs of men*, is what brings true significance to life. As the verses unfold in this chapter we see an amazing transition in King Nebuchadnezzar. He journeys from his boasting in verse 30, *Is not this great Babylon, that I have built for a royal dwelling by my mighty power and for the honor of my majesty?*, to concluding with these words, *Now I, Nebuchadnezzar, praise and extol and honor the King of heaven, all of whose works are truth, and His ways justice. And those who walk in pride He is able to put down.* (Dan. 4:37) What happened? These are the last words of one of the most ingenious, creative, productive and successful men who has ever lived. He left us his legacy here. Do you see it? He passed from successful to significance and in this one chapter shows us the way to this valuable discovery of life.

What will it be for us? We have a choice. We can base our self worth on success, our ability to achieve or to please others. Or, we can base it upon significance, our sense of self worth that's found in our identity with the Lord Jesus Christ who set us apart before he formed us in the womb. We can pick one of two goals in life. We can search for significance, or we can search for success. In this volume we have heard from Daniel, we have heard from Shadrach, Meshach, and Abednego, and now it is time for us to hear from King Nebuchadnezzar himself. He has quite a testimony to share with us. He knows from experience the way from success to significance. He says two simple things to us. The way down is up and, the way up is down.

Chapter 10

The way down is up

Dan. 4:1-31

The way down is up. Most of our current, contemporary culture does not think this is true. They think the way up is up. But Nebuchadnezzar testifies to us in this chapter that indeed, the way down is up — *is this not the great Babylon that I have built for a royal dwelling by my mighty power and for the honor of my majesty?* (Dan. 4:30) But our Lord reminds us that *whoever exalts himself will be humbled.* (Matt. 23:12) It was his way of saying the way down is up. Nebuchadnezzar was a man geared and governed by the success syndrome for most of his life. The more he had, the more he craved. In the third chapter of Daniel we see him building a golden image of himself with his prideful desire to have everyone bow down to worship his image. He ruled not only his nation but also himself by pride and was convinced that the way up was up for most of his life. That is, until he had a confrontation with the living God.

The introduction to Chapter 4 is in fact the conclusion. *Nebuchadnezzar the king, To all peoples, nations, and languages that dwell in all the earth: Peace be multiplied to you. I thought it good to declare the signs and wonders that the Most High God has worked for me*. (Dan. 4:1-3) These words actually came after his humbling and humiliating ordeal in Daniel Chapter 4. This chapter really reveals to us his personal testimony. He speaks of *peace* in Daniel 4:1. One thinks immediately of Paul's own epistles. These are the words of a man who's been transformed. Remember, this is the same man who spent his life at war. He conquered one nation after another after another. He engaged in one war after another. This is the same man who had taken millions of slaves for the sole purpose of building a world empire to satisfy his own pride in his own search for success. This is also the same man who uprooted families and nations, all to satisfy his own prideful success. This is the same man who in a rage of anger heated the fiery furnace seven times hotter than normal for the three Hebrew young men. This is the same man we read about in II Kings Chapter 25 who slew King Zedekiah's sons in front of him and then put out Zedekiah's own eyes so that the last thing he ever saw was the death of his boys. This is the man who stepped over anyone and anything to satisfy his own pride. This is the man that thought the way up was up in his search for success. Now we hear him speaking of peace.

What happened? In Daniel Chapter 4 Nebuchadnezzar made a journey from success to significance. But, he had to learn his lesson the hard way. He says to us across the centuries today that the way down is up. Note his testimony, *I thought it good to declare the signs and wonders that the most high God has worked for me.* (Dan. 4:2) He gave credit where credit was due. God had done these wonderful things. He goes on to say, *How great are His signs, and how mighty His wonders! His kingdom is an everlasting kingdom, and his dominion is from generation to generation.* (Dan. 4:2-3) Nebuchadnezzar had finally realized that the Babylonian kingdom was only temporary. God was in control and it is His kingdom that is the only everlasting kingdom. Now he wants the whole world to know what God had done for him.

What happened? How did it happen? Let's trace together Nebuchadnezzar's own journey from success to significance. It all began in verse 4—*I, Nebuchadnezzar, was at rest in my house and flourishing in my palace.* Look at him. He is at rest. He is *flourishing*. This is the only time this Aramaic word is used in the Bible. It corresponds to the word meaning *green* or *to grow* luxuriantly. Nebuchadnezzar was testifying that his kingdom was the epitome of success. I can almost see him now. His feet are propped up on his desk. He says, "I've got it made!" He is flourishing. He leans back, dozes off to sleep, and has a dream. His dream frightens him. The dream was of a tree that grew until it was very big and spreading its branches. It was an awesome sight. Then it was cut down and hauled off. However, the stump of the tree was left. A band of iron and brass kept it from being uprooted.

Troubled by this dream Nebuchadnezzar needs an interpreter. So he calls in the same losers that failed to interpret his dream in the second chapter of Daniel. A man ruled by pride and worldly success never learns. He is destined to repeat the same mistakes. None of Nebuchadnezzar's "wise men" could interpret the dream. But Daniel comes through with the interpretation. He has some good news and some bad news for the king. The good news is that the king is great and strong like the mighty tree of his dream. But then came the bad news. He is going to be cut down. Daniel left no doubt that this tree was Nebuchadnezzar himself. He says, *The tree that you saw…it is you, O king, who have grown and become strong…* (Dan. 4:20-22)

Daniel's interpretation was that this mighty tree will fall. However, it will not die. It will spring to life again. This tree describes a man who would lose all reason and behave like an animal for a period of time. He will be driven from men and his *dwelling will be with the beast of the field and they shall make you eat grass like oxen.* (Dan. 4:25) Daniel's interpretation revealed to Nebuchadnezzar that he was about to lose his mind. He would go through temporary insanity after which he would be restored to his sanity and to his kingdom. Nebuchadnezzar was about to find out the hard way that the way down is up. God was about to reveal the truth that *the Most High rules in the kingdom of men…* (Dan. 4:25) God has His own way of moving us from success to significance. The kingdoms of men all rise and fall but the Most High rules in the kingdom of men.

Daniel begins to plead with King Nebuchadnezzar. *Therefore, O King, let my advice be acceptable to you; break off your sins by being righteous and your iniquities by showing mercy to the poor. Perhaps there may be a lengthening of your prosperity.* (Dan. 4:27) Daniel warned Nebuchadnezzar that if he did not break from his sin he would ultimately be broken by his sin. Our culture today is filled with broken, wasted lives and people who refuse to break away from their sins. King Nebuchadnezzar was certainly successful by the world's standards, but it was a success without any real significance in life. It is so much better to break from our sin than to be broken by our sin. I've seen men and women from all walks of life broken by their sin. I've been with men who once were so proud and heard them weep when they lost their family to their own pride or promiscuity. If only they had broken from their sin. Now, they were broken by it. They, like Nebuchadnezzar, learned that *the Most High rules in the kingdom of men.*

For those who are caught up in the success syndrome of today's contemporary culture and think the way up is up, this is a warning. For those who do whatever they have to do to become successful, Daniel's warning to Nebuchadnezzar is as fresh to you today — *break off your sins*. Daniel's challenge was for Nebuchadnezzar to practice righteousness and show mercy. That is, get into a right relationship with God and with man.

Judgment did not fall on King Nebuchadnezzar at once. Daniel 4:29 tells us that 12 months passed. God's grace was extended to him for 12 months, the whole year. But

Nebuchadnezzar did not do anything about it. In fact, he strutted like a proud peacock on the roof of his palace saying, *Is not this the great Babylon, that I have built for a royal dwelling by my mighty power and for the honor of my majesty?* (Dan. 4:30) And then judgment came suddenly. When he least expected it, Nebuchadnezzar found out that the way down was up. *While the word was still in the king's mouth, a voice fell from heaven: King Nebuchadnezzar to you it is spoken: the kingdom has departed from you!* (Dan. 4:31) Yes, our Lord reminds us that whoever exalts himself will be humbled. Since Nebuchadnezzar would not break from his sin, we find him broken by it. He speaks across the centuries to bear testimony to us today. He thought the way up was up. But he was wrong. As he put it, *those who walk in pride He is able to put down.* (Dan. 4:37) The way down is up!

Chapter 11

The way up is down

Dan. 4:31-37

Success says, *Is not this great Babylon that I have built for a royal dwelling by my mighty power and for the honor of my majesty?* (Dan. 4:29) Significance says, *I Nebuchadnezzar, lifted my eyes to heaven, and my understanding returned to me; and I blessed the most high and praised and honored Him who lives forever…all of His works are true and His ways justice. And those who walk in pride He is able to put down.* (Dan. 4:34-37) Yes, the way up is really down! He that truly humbles himself will eventually be exalted.

The way to true success in life is through the search for significance. James, in the New Testament, reminds us that, *God resists the proud…* (James 4:6) He chooses a Greek word, which we translate *resist,* that means to battle against or to oppose. It is a military term. In other words, God is set against the proud. God has His own way of taking a stand against the proud. On the journey to significance we find that not only is the way up down, but also the way down is up.

The narrative unfolds with King Nebuchadnezzar stepping out on his roof and looking over the city he had built. Its walls were 40 feet across and 80 feet high and extended for 15 miles. The city contained 50 temples with a temple built in pyramid form 600 feet high with a statue on top extending almost another 50 feet. There were palaces and hanging gardens. The beautiful Euphrates wound its way through the city. What a sight! It is said there was never a city before or after Babylon quite like it. As Nebuchadnezzar looks over this view he exclaims, *Is not this the great Babylon that I have built for a royal dwelling by my mighty power and for the honor of my majesty?* (Dan. 4:30) There are a lot of people in our contemporary culture today who have this attitude. They think they are really in control and running their own lives. In their own way they're exclaiming, "Is not this the great Babylon which I have built?" Remember what Nebuchadnezzar had just seen in Daniel Chapter 3. He had seen God deliver the three Hebrew young men from the burning fiery furnace. He exclaimed, *Blessed be the God of Shadrach, Meshach, and Abednego who sent his Angel and delivered his servants who trusted in Him…There is no other God who can deliver like this.* (Dan. 3:28-29) But talk is cheap. King Nebuchadnezzar forgot about this and went on his way unchanged like so many today.

As he stood on his rooftop boasting about the great Babylon he had built, his demise came suddenly. In the words of Scripture, *While the word was still in the king's mouth, a voice fell from heaven: King Nebuchadnezzar, to you it is spoken: the kingdom is departed from you!* (Dan. 4:31) Yes, the way down is up. Nebuchadnezzar had built his great wall. He had shut out his enemies. He was at rest. He was flourishing. He was prancing around the palace in self-exaltation. He had shut everyone out…except the Lord God who *rules in the kingdom of men.* (Dan. 4:32) God's judgment fell upon Nebuchadnezzar. It is a horrible thing to see. This once proud king ended up on all fours walking around like an animal. He lost his mind. The Bible tells us he was eating grass like an animal. Before he was clothed in regal robes and now he wallows in insanity. After awhile his hair begins to mat together and his nails become like *birds' claws.*

It happened while he spoke. God warns a man for months, maybe years. He gives him time to repent. Then suddenly judgment falls. The Bible says, *He who is often rebuked, and hardens his neck, will suddenly be destroyed, and that without remedy.* (Prov. 29:1) God's judgment fell upon Nebuchadnezzar suddenly. This is the way it happens. *Pride goes before destruction, and a haughty spirit before a fall.* (Prov. 16:18) God's grace was extended for several months to Nebuchadnezzar but he did nothing about it. It was pride that caused Lucifer to be cast out of heaven. (Isa. 14:12-15) Yes, the way down is up. It was pride that caused Adam and Eve to fall from Eden's Garden. And, it was pride that caused Nebuchadnezzar to end up in the shape he was. And, it is that same pride that causes so many men and women in our contemporary culture, who think they're indestructible, to find out that the way down is up.

But the mighty matchless monarch gets a second chance. (Dan. 4:34-37) The one who conquered the world now humbles himself. The old arrogance is now gone. The old egotistical pride has left. What a scene as he humbles himself and glorifies the living God. The arrogance of Daniel 4:30 is replaced with the adoration of Daniel 4:34, *I lifted my eyes to heaven and my understanding returned to me: and I blessed the Most High and praised and honored Him who is forever.* The verbs in verse 34 indicate a continuous action. That is, this attitude became a lifestyle for King Nebuchadnezzar. He continued to bless God, and to praise and honor Him habitually for the rest of his life. Pride had been replaced with praise. *Now I, Nebuchadnezzar, praise and extol and honor the King of heaven, all of whose works are true, and His ways justice. And those who walk in pride He is able to put down.* (Dan. 4:37) Yes, he's saying to us that the way up is really down.

The first thing Nebuchadnezzar did in his journey to significance was to lift his eyes to heaven. (Dan. 4:34) Crisis experiences of life can point us to God if we will allow them to do so. The Psalmist said, *Before I was afflicted I went astray, but now I keep your word. You are good, and do good; teach me Your statutes.* (Ps. 119:67-68)

Nebuchadnezzar's testimony is that *my reason returned to me…* His reign also returned to him, *for the glory of my kingdom.* His reputation returned to him, *I was restored to my kingdom and excellent majesty was added to me.* (Dan. 4:36)

God has a way of keeping His promises. In the interpretation of Nebuchadnezzar's dream Daniel reminded the king that the tree would not be completely destroyed but the stump and the roots of the tree would remain so that *your kingdom shall be restored to you after you come to know that Heaven rules.* (Dan. 4:26) God is being faithful to his word.

King Nebuchadnezzar's last words were recorded for all prosperity. *Now I, Nebuchadnezzar, praise and extol and honor the King of heaven, all of whose works are truth, and His ways justice. And those who walk in pride He is able to put down.* (Dan. 4:37) These are his last words and we never hear from him again. He leaves us his legacy — *those who walk in pride He is able to put down.* Yes, the way down is up, but the way up is down!

The search for significance is one of the most basic pursuits of life, even more so than the pursuit of money and pleasure. We are all involved in a constant search for significance. Many of us think significance is found in what our culture calls success. Many in our world today are searching for significance in all the wrong places. We think if we can just do something better than anyone else it will bring us significance. If we can just close more deals, get more acceptance, perform at a higher level, win more legal cases, and on and on. This search permeates our current culture in America. The very first page of the Bible reveals that we are people of significance. Why? Because we were created by God. We are not part of some random evolutionary cycle. Significance is something that is ours from the beginning. Most all of our attempts to regain significance today are futile because most men and women are searching in the wrong place. Significance is found in God, not in us.

Man did not always struggle with this halting feeling that he was insignificant. We were created with significance! An interesting thing happened on the sixth day of creation. All through the early verses of Genesis God was involved in His creative activity. The fact that you were the last thing He created shows you are the most significant thing of his creation. He crowned all his creation by creating you and me. (Gen. 1:23-27)

The Bible says, *And the Lord formed man of the dust of the ground and breathed into his nostrils the breath of life; and man became a living being.* (Gen. 2:7) Not only did God create you last of all creation, but differently. He had been about what we call *fiat* creation. That is, God spoke and it was so. He speaks the world and all His other creation into existence with the spoken word. Then He gets to you and me and a change takes place. He did not speak us into existence. He could have, but He did not. He took existing material that He had, the dust of the ground, and *formed* man. This word *formed* in Genesis 2:7 is the same word that is used for the potter and the clay in other places in the Old Testament. That is, God himself became an artisan. He was about the business of meticulously shaping man. And then He gave us animation by breathing into us the breathe of life. Can you see this great Creator God hovering over us in this creative process? Everything else He spoke into existence. But He took time and effort when He began to work on you. We are different than all the other created order. We have significance! We are unique. We were created in the image of God. That is, He is a spirit and those who worship Him worship Him in spirit and in truth. We have significance. It is not found in what we accomplish or in our abilities. It is found all the way back in the creation process. He placed us in a garden and gave us dominion over it.

If we are so significant then why do we not sense it? Because we lost our significance. That is why we are on a search for it today. And where did we lose it? All one need do is read Genesis Chapter 3 to find out. Satan is not always in diabolical form. God created him as an angel of light. He too had significance. But he thought the way up was up and said, *I will be like the Most High.* (Isa. 12:14) He sounds a bit like King Nebuchadnezzar, doesn't he? Then he invaded our lives in the Garden of Eden. Pride entered the picture. We bought in to it and in so doing we lost our significance. Ever since then men and women have been searching for significance that was lost. We've looked for it in anything and everything the world has to offer. Our loss of significance is directly related to our loss of identity and relationship with our Creator.

Paul wrote about this in Romans 5:12 — *...through one man sin entered the world and death through sin and thus that death spread to all men for all sinned.* Everyone born since Adam and Eve has been born spiritually dead. You may gain all the material things that life can afford. You may have homes and cars and clothes and jewelry. But having all those things you can still be longing for significance. Some of us in our contemporary culture think, "If I could just gain wealth I'd find significance." King Nebuchadnezzar was wealthy. He had power. He had it all. Like Solomon he, too, found out that it was all vanity. Solomon concluded that without a relationship with the Creator, everything under the sun was insignificant. There is no end to the search of significance unless it ends in your relationship with God.

We began in the Garden with significance. But we lost it. And, we have been on a search ever since. Men and women all around us are searching for significance in life. Only God can restore it. Yes, *the Most High rules in the kingdom of men…* (Dan. 4:17) God made provision for us through the Lord Jesus Christ. The search for significance is not found in seven habits of successful living or winning friends and influencing people or of any of the modern, positive-thinking techniques. Significance is only found in our relationship with the Lord Jesus Christ. The way up is still down, to humble ourselves before God.

God gives us a plan to recover the significance we once had and lost. What is it? Jesus Christ came to this earth to restore our lost heritage. In fact, He is the one on a search today. He set aside his glory. He emptied Himself. He clothed himself with human flesh. And He who knew no sin became sin for us that we might become the righteousness of God in Him. He took our sin on Calvary's cross that we might take His righteousness. He died our death that we might live His life. If we're looking for significance today we'll never find it looking horizontally. King Nebuchadnezzar lifted up his eyes to heaven. Our search for significance can be over today. We can reclaim at the foot of a Roman cross what we once had and lost.

Daniel is teaching us how to thrive in a culture that's foreign to our value system and truth claims. Through the pages of this volume he has challenged us to not give up, to not give in, and to not give out. His three Hebrew friends have challenged us to learn to live with pressure, principle, perspective, and protection. Now, King Nebuchadnezzar himself testifies to us that the way down is up and the way up is down.

Daniel Chapter 4 leaves us with a word about pride . . .*those who walk in pride He is able to put down.* (Dan. 4:37) God hates the proud. In fact, the Bible says God resists the proud. Pride leads to a parade of sins which God tells us in Proverbs 6:16 that He hates. Daniel also leaves us with a word about procrastination. *At the end of the twelve months he was walking about the royal palace of Babylon.* (Dan. 4:29) Nebuchadnezzar reminds us that there's a danger of forgetting God in the midst of long continued blessings and unheeded warnings.

Not only is there a word about pride and procrastination but there's also a word about presumption to be found here. Nebuchadnezzar says, *is not this the great Babylon that I have built for a royal dwelling by my mighty power and for the honor of my majesty?* (Dan. 4:30) There will not always be adequate time to make things right. We presume there will be, but there will not be. If we don't break from our sin we will most likely be broken by it.

Finally, there's a word about providence. Yes, *the Most High rules in the kingdom of men…* (Dan. 4:17) One way or another God will ultimately show us all that He is in control.

If we are ever going to address our culture today we must learn some valuable lessons. The way down is up. But thank God, the way up is down! Our culture is waiting to see us practice what we preach. And, they need to be reminded that *those who walk in pride He is able to put down.*

Part V

God and graffiti — The handwriting is on the wall

Throughout human history, public walls have been used to communicate various ideas from political dissent to love messages to purely artistic endeavors. Our own culture has expanded and enhanced this age-old art form we commonly refer to as "graffiti." The word finds its origin in ancient Rome. It is the plural of *graffito*, which means "to scratch." It commonly refers to drawing on a wall in such a way as to be seen by the public to communicate a particular message. The word "graffiti" finds its roots in writing on the walls of the ruins of ancient Pompeii and Rome around 50 B.C.

Graffiti is a worldwide phenomenon. It communicates its message around the globe. Who of us can forget the tearing down of the Berlin Wall in 1990? As we watched on our television screens as it came tumbling down we noted that it was filled with graffiti on its western side. For years this 15-foot high and over 100-mile long wall had borne messages to the world of a long hoped-for freedom. During the days of the first *intifadeh* in 1987 in Jerusalem, the old city walls of the Arab section were filled with graffiti. Palestinian flags with their red, green and black colors were on walls all over East Jerusalem. In our own city of Dallas, the city fathers have just declared a particular underpass in the Deep Ellum section of the city as an historical landmark because of its graffiti-filled walls. Modern billboards that line the highways of America find their roots in graffiti art. Graffiti's new turf today is on the Internet.

The original graffiti artist is found in the fifth chapter of Daniel. We must go back beyond Pompeii and back beyond Rome. In fact, we must go back another five centuries to ancient Babylon. There we find the original graffiti on the wall of the banquet hall in King Belshazzar's palace. As we transition from the fourth chapter of Daniel to the fifth, we need to be reminded that 20 years have passed. King Nebuchadnezzar is off the scene. He has been succeeded by his son who was assassinated by his brother-in-law who in turn ruled for four years and then lost his own life in battle. He was followed by two rulers, one of whom, Nabonidus and his son Belshazzar, ruled briefly as co-regents. Thus, in this chapter we journey back to Babylon to an evening at a drunken orgy hosted by King Belshazzar. As the Babylonians blasphemed and partied, a strange thing happened, *In the same hour the fingers of a man's hand appeared and wrote opposite the lamp stand on the plaster of the wall of the king's palace; and the king saw the part of the hand that wrote.* (Dan. 5:5) The inscription that was written was *mene, tekel, upharsin*. The handwriting was on the wall!

The finger that wrote on Belshazzar's palace wall was the finger of God. He had a message to communicate for all the people to see so he wrote it on a large plaster wall. What did this strange message seem to convey? Daniel, now almost 90 years of age, is once again summoned to the banquet hall for an interpretation. He reveals the writing on the wall: *And this is the inscription that was written: MENE, MENE, TEKEL, UPHARSIN. This is the interpretation of each word. MENE: God has numbered your kingdom, and finished it; TEKEL: You have been weighed in the balances, and found wanting; PERES: Your kingdom has been divided, and given to the Medes and Persians.* (Dan. 5:25-28) And, did it ever come true! *Mene* is an Aramaic noun from a verb meaning "to number." It means your number is up, you're finished, your time has run out, it's over. *Tekel* is a noun from a verb meaning to weigh as one might weigh on a scale. Solomon reminds us that *All the ways of a man are pure in his own eyes, but the Lord weighs the spirits.* (Prov.16:2) Belshazzar was weighed upon that scale that night and he was found wanting. *Upharsin* is a noun from a verb that means to break into, to separate or to divide. Not only were Belshazzar's days numbered and not only was he weighed and found wanting, but he was to be separated.

These three words proclaim the destiny of all those without Christ. They reveal the ultimate end of opportunity, the judgment that comes when we're judged on the scales of the righteous demands of the law and found wanting, and the separation that comes throughout eternity. Belshazzar had come to the end of the number of days, he was weighed and found wanting, and he was soon to be separated from all he knew and loved. These are three haunting words. This handwriting on the wall is still there today. The problem is that some of us do not see it. Our own days are numbered. Some of us are weighed in God's balance and if we do not exchange our own righteousness for the righteousness of Christ we too will be found wanting and separated forever.

God and graffiti. The handwriting is on the wall. These same fingers had written before and they will write again. When God sent the plagues upon ancient Egypt, the Pharaoh's counselor came to him after the plague of the lice and exclaimed, *This is the finger of God.* (Ex. 8:19) When Moses was in the wilderness God gave him the two tablets of the testimony of the law, tablets of stone written with the *finger of God.* (Ex. 31:18) Centuries later God came and clothed Himself in human flesh and once again we would read that when He was confronted with a woman in adultery who was hovered over by self-righteous Pharisees, *Jesus stooped down and wrote on the ground with his finger…* (John 8:6) That evening, in Babylon, God visited Belshazzar's drunken orgy and left the handwriting on the wall for all to see. The Lord Himself came to Belshazzar's feast and wrote a message of judgment on the wall. We need to be reminded that His handwriting is still on the wall today as a warning to our own culture. *Mene, mene, tekel, upharsin* is written across our culture today.

Our narrative in Daniel Chapter 5 unfolds some 70 years following the events of Chapter 1 when Daniel was taken into Babylonian captivity as a teenager. He is well up into his eighties. King Nebuchadnezzar has been gone for 20 years. He died leaving us his legacy in the last words of Daniel 4:37 — *Now I, Nebuchadnezzar, praise and extol and honor the King of heaven all of whose works are truth and His ways are justice. And those who walk in pride He is able to bring down.* This is his lasting legacy. We now are introduced to the last king of Babylon, a man by the name of Belshazzar. He is the grandson of King Nebuchadnezzar and co-regent of the nation with his father Nabonidus. As the chapter begins we find the fabulous city of Babylon besieged by the armies of the Medes and Persians under the able leadership of Cyrus. However, the great tragedy was that Babylon was crumbling from within at the same time.

While the city of Babylon was besieged by the great armies of the Medes and the Persians, King Belshazzar was feasting. He should have been fasting. He was blind and belligerent. He called a thousand of the nobles of Babylon to a great party in the royal hall. There was wine, women and song. This was the office party to beat all office parties. All the concubines were there. The orgies which ensued during these godless feasts should not be properly described in a book such as this. They were as perverted and sick as much of what is taking place in the perversion of our contemporary culture.

As the party got into full swing and the crowd became more and more intoxicated, Belshazzar sent for the gold vessels which had been brought to Babylon from the temple in Jerusalem when King Nebuchadnezzar conquered the Southern Kingdom. For 70 years these sacred utensils which had been used in the worship of the living God in the temple in Jerusalem had been in safe storage in Babylon. In his folly, King Belshazzar filled them with drink and mocked the living God by drinking from them. His drunkenness and sexual perversion were not enough, now he was blaspheming the true and living God. It was at this point, *in the same hour* (Dan. 5:5), that a man's hand began to write graffiti on the wall of the royal hall.

At once the drinking, feasting, and illicit sex stopped. A deathly silence filled the hall. Fear swept over the crowd in waves. King Belshazzar's response is recorded in Daniel 5:6 — *Then the king's countenance changed, and his thoughts troubled him, so that the joints of his hips were loosened and his knees knocked against each other.* His face, which moments earlier had been red with wine, is now ashen white. Fear gripped his hardened heart. His eyes, which had been squinting moments earlier, were now wide open. His lips were quivering and his heart was beating out of his chest. His knees were knocking. Yes, *it is a fearful thing to fall into the hands of the living God.* (Heb.10:31) The handwriting is on the wall in our own culture today.

What did King Belshazzar do? *The king cried aloud to bring in the astrologers, the Chaldeans, the soothsayers. The king spoke to the wise men of Babylon, whoever reads this writing and tells me its interpretation shall be clothed with purple and shall have a chain of gold around his neck; and he shall be the third ruler in the kingdom.* (Dan. 5:7) Here we go again. He brings in the same old losers that his predecessors had known. Those that claim to have the wisdom of this world do not have the answers for the heart of man when the handwriting is on the wall. The tragedy of our culture today is that so many do the same thing. That is, they run to people who, in the final analysis, bring no real help. Now King Belshazzar was *greatly troubled.* (Dan. 7:28)

Next, the Queen Mother appears. She reminds Belshazzar that there is a man *in your kingdom in whom is the spirit of the holy God.* (Dan. 5:11) Isn't this our culture's greatest need? God is still looking for a man to make known His message to cultures such as ours and to do so without fear or favor. He is searching for a man, like Daniel, in whom the spirit of God dwells, to stand in the gap. He is searching for one who would dare to be a Daniel in our current contemporary culture. Daniel is brought into the hall and he lays out the message. He does not water it down. He puts it like this: *And this is the inscription that was written: MENE, MENE, TEKEL, UPHARSIN. This is the interpretation of each word. MENE: God has numbered your kingdom, and finished it; TEKEL: You have been weighed in the balances, and found wanting; PERES: Your kingdom has been divided, and given to the Medes and Persians.* (Dan. 5:25-28)

This brings us to a poignant question. Where are God's men who are doing this today? Where are those men and women in whom the spirit of God dwells, who tell it like it is without watering it down? So many today are more interested in getting an invitation to King Belshazzar's feast and being recognized as "one of the boys" than they are in speaking the truth, especially when it means speaking the truth of God's judgment.

Daniel's was a message of judgment. *Mene, tekel, upharsin!* Every book of the Bible carries a warning of judgment to come. The strange thing that is taking place in our culture today is that this book with warnings of judgment on virtually every page is seldom mentioned in the pulpit. Where are the Daniels today, taking the word from the finger of God and saying to the people, "*Mene, tekel, upharsin* — your days are numbered, you'll be weighed in the scale and found wanting, you'll be separated forever"? It has been years since many people in churches have heard a syllable spoken like that from the pulpit regarding the coming judgment of God. The job of the preacher is not to tell men and women what they want to hear but to take the message from the finger of God and lay it out before the people without fear or favor. It is to speak the truth in love. There have been a couple of generations raised in American churches today who have heard nothing of the judgment of God and know nothing of the fear of God.

God himself records the final day of the kingdom of Babylon. *That very night Belshazzar, king of the Chaldeans, was slain. And Darius the Mede received the kingdom, being 62 years old.* (Dan. 5:30-31) Thus we read of the end of the great Babylonian Empire. God kept His word and that night the head of gold became the chest of silver (Dan. 2:32-35).

The Medes and Persian broke the Babylonian supremacy just as God had prophesied and predicted in His Holy Word.

As we journey together through these first six chapters of Daniel we are learning much about how to live in the midst of a pagan culture that is foreign to our own faith claims and value systems. As Daniel Chapter 5 unfolds before us we find so many blatant and obvious parallels to our own culture. It shows that a culture like ours is doomed without a massive spiritual awakening and turning to God. Simply making a few affirmations in God's direction as King Nebuchadnezzar did in Chapters 3 and 4 will not suffice. The handwriting is on the wall today. The church must step out of ancient Babylon with its fading pageantry and false pride and bring this unchanging truth into confrontation with our culture.

How do we confront our culture? After all, the handwriting is on the wall today. And, just like Babylon, our world cannot interpret it. Our "kings" bring in the best advisers but so many of them are blind to the truth of the writing of the finger of God. How do we engage our culture? By standing tall like Daniel. Where is Daniel? He is in their midst, on their turf, delivering God's message to them. The handwriting is on the wall today. We have the Word of God from His own finger and yet we seldom share it in a loving way in which we present His message of *mene, tekel, upharsin.* Why? Perhaps we're obsessed with being accepted, by getting invitations to our own banquets, by being consumed with trying to get others to think well of us.

Daniel is saying to us across the centuries today, "Deliver God's message!" Never underestimate the power of one good and godly life with character, integrity and courage to say that the handwriting is on the wall. *Mene, tekel, upharsin.* Your days are numbered, you're weighed in the balance and found wanting, you'll be separated forever.

The church of Jesus Christ in our current, contemporary culture desperately needs to speak the message at four particular points today. As the fifth chapter of Daniel unfolds before us, the handwriting is on the wall. What is God saying? God is speaking to the culture in America today at the point of our pride, at the point of our presumption, at the point of our promiscuity, and at the point of our perversion. Yes, unless we repent it will be *mene, tekel, upharsin* for us as well.

Chapter 12

God is speaking to us at the point of our pride

Dan. 5:20-23

King Belshazzar's problem, like so many of us in our culture today, was that he had forgotten some valuable lessons from the past. Not the least of these lessons was the one that Nebuchadnezzar mentioned, *and those who walk in pride He is able to put down.* (Dan. 4:37) What is pride? Daniel gives us a very pertinent insight in Chapter 5, verse 23, *And you have lifted yourself up against the Lord of heaven.* The phrase *lifted yourself up* means to boast, to elevate or to lift one's self up above the rest. This is exactly what Belshazzar was doing. He was busy boasting about himself. Like King Nebuchadnezzar before him who once asked, *Is not this the great Babylon which I have built?*, Belshazzar elevated himself in like manner.

Pride always brings a fall. God has His own ways of putting down those who walk in pride. At the very top of the list of those things which God hates is pride. Ask Lucifer if those who walk in pride are not put down. Ask Adam and Eve if those who begin to walk in pride are not put down. Ask King David the same question.

Perhaps no one can testify to this more than Simon Peter. Peter, once so brash and bold, was warned by Jesus that *Satan has asked for you that he might sift you as wheat. But I have prayed for you, that your faith shall not fail...* (Luke 22:31-32) Peter responded by saying, *Lord, I am ready to go with you, both to prison and to death.* (Luke 22:33) He was so pridefully confident in his self-determination. But Jesus knew better. He replied, *I tell you, Peter, the rooster shall not crow this day before you will deny three times that you know Me.* (Luke 22:34)

If we were to ask a dozen Christians who their favorite apostle is, the majority of them would probably say Simon Peter. Perhaps the reason is that he is so intensely human. He is just like so many of us in our culture today: impulsive and impetuous. Clearly, Simon Peter did not expect to deny the Lord. In spite of Christ's clear warning, turning his back on the Lord Jesus Christ must have been the farthest thing from his mind. But then, none of us deliberately intend to indulge in a spiritual downfall as a result of our own pride. Most of the time we, like Simon Peter, are blinded to the fact of it.

Peter's own failure began with pride. Jesus warned Peter in the gentlest and most compassionate manner imaginable to not trust in himself and let pride rule his life. So, what was Peter's response? He said, Lord, *I'm ready to go with you.* It doesn't matter where. If it's prison I'll be with you. I can handle it — whatever it might be. Like Simon Peter, Nebuchadnezzar, Belshazzar or anyone else, step one on our spiritual downgrade is a prideful over-confidence in the flesh. It is a dangerous thing to be so sure of ourselves, yet it is almost as if we are intent on training people to flaunt confidence in the flesh by redoubling our efforts to teach self-esteem, self-confidence, self-reliance, and self-actualization.

Peter's pride led to his own prayerlessness. We remember he could not even stay awake with our Lord when He prayed in Gethsemane's garden. It is pride that resulted in prayerlessness which brought forth presumption. The next thing we see Simon Peter doing is striking off the right ear of the servant of the high priest in the garden. Pride leads us to do all sorts of irrational, presumptuous things. This presumption then led to a sort of paranoia. After Jesus' arrest we find that Peter *followed at a distance.* (Luke 22:54) Next came peer pressure. We find him sitting next to a fire succumbing to the peer pressure around him and denying he knew our Lord. Then things went from bad to worse. After failing the peer pressure, a paralysis set in. His bold allegiance of just a few hours earlier suddenly faded into the background of his consciousness. This brought about the next step in his downgrade. It was perjury. Open denial. Lying. *I never knew the man.* Peter's tragic fall was centered in his own pride.

God is speaking to our own contemporary culture today at the point of our pride. This nation that once honored God so unashamedly and openly and credited Him with our blessing and our success has today followed the same pathway. Is the handwriting on the wall of our western culture today? *Mene, tekel, upharsin.* God is weighing our hearts and speaking to us at the point of our pride.

Chapter 13

God is speaking to us at the point of our presumption

Dan. 5:1

So Belshazzar the king made a great feast for a thousand of his lords which resulted in a giant, drunken orgy. However, at the same time, just outside the city walls the Medes and Persians were camped out. Talk about presumption. Belshazzar was convinced that Babylon was indestructible. Everywhere one walked atop the 60 miles of walls that encompassed the great city of Babylon one could see the enemy. But what did Belshazzar care? The walls were so high and so thick they were impossible to penetrate. Historians tell us there were supplies in the city that could last for up to 20 years.

So what did Belshazzar do? He threw a big party! He invited a thousand guests to his drunken orgy. His confidence was in the physical, in his seemingly impregnable city. So he continued to party when destruction was at the door. Can we hear God speaking to us at the point of our own presumption in our culture today as we see this scene unfold?

Ironically, it is often in those times when a man feels himself most secure in his own strength that personal peril is most imminent. We are reminded of the rich, young fool about whom Jesus spoke in Luke Chapter 12:16. The young man said, *I will say to my soul, "Soul, you have many goods laid up for many years; take your ease; eat, drink, and be merry..."* Unfortunately, it was that very night that his soul was required of him! While Cyrus' army was besieging the city, King Belshazzar threw a wild party thinking himself indestructible. At the moment of his greatest danger his presumption led him to party his troubles away. At least that's what he thought!

This is a picture of many of those in our current contemporary culture who should know better. Many have gotten away with forgetting God for so long they think it will last forever. How foolish. Belshazzar was too blind and drunken by his own success to realize that the strength of the kingdom or an individual is never on the outside but it's on the inside. Babylon did not fall because the Medes and Persians had encompassed the city but because they had become so corrupt and presumptuous on the inside.

We are living in a culture that is rotting on the inside. What we see in Babylon is repeated in so many ways in our western world. Oh, every once in a while we hear our own king say something about God like Nebuchadnezzar did in Chapter 3 or Chapter 4. But, we have our own way of going on in the same ungodliness. For a few days in the aftermath of the September 11th tragedy it seemed as though people were turning back to God. Churches were filled. Hearts were open and softened. But it only took a few weeks for the same old thought processes to take hold again. Some of us think the walls around America are impregnable. After all, the Cold War is over. Russia no longer seems to be a threat. At this writing we're touted across the world as being the only world power of our day. Could it be that God is speaking to us at the very point of our own presumption?

God may be saying the same thing to us today that he said to the Babylonians and that he said to the Corinthians, *Let him who thinks he stands take heed lest he fall.* (I Cor. 10:12) So many in our culture today are presuming on so many things. We think we're bulletproof. Some of us think we can keep on in the same unfaithfulness and not be caught. God is speaking to us at the point of our presumption.

Yes, the handwriting is on the wall for our culture. *Mene, tekel, upharsin.* Our days are numbered. God is weighing our hearts, there is a reckoning day coming. As he did to the Babylonians, God continues to speak to us at the point of our pride and the point of our presumption.

Chapter 14

God is speaking to us at the point of our promiscuity

Dan. 5:2

Babylonian culture was filled with what the Old Testament politely describes as "concubines." These were women who were kept for the purpose of sexual gratification or additional procreation. American culture, like Babylonian culture before it, has been given over to promiscuity. Sexual permissiveness and sexual perversion is rampant in our culture. God is speaking to us not only at the point of our pride and presumption, but at the point of our promiscuity.

Babylonian culture collapsed in the fifth chapter of Daniel. They felt so secure, but they crumbled from within. The Babylonians made four major mistakes. They lost all sense of *remembrance*. Belshazzar had forgotten the lessons King

Nebuchadnezzar had learned. They lost all sense of *reality*. They thought they were invincible and did not face reality. They lost all sense of *restraint*. They became increasingly morally degenerate. They lost all sense of *respect*. Nothing was sacred to them any more. These are the same four danger signs in our contemporary culture as God doesn't just speak, but shouts to us at the point of our own promiscuity.

We, too, have lost a sense of remembrance. Belshazzar had forgotten the valuable lessons that were learned in the past. Pride causes this. Daniel gave us a pertinent insight into it when he said to Belshazzar, *and you have lifted yourself up against the Lord of heaven.* (Dan. 5:23) Our own nation which once honored God so unashamedly and credited Him with our blessings and successes seems today to have lost a bit of our sense of remembrance. During the days of World War I President Woodrow Wilson put it like this — "A nation that does not remember what it was yesterday does not know what it is today, nor what it is trying to do. We are about a futile thing if we do not know where we came from nor what we've been about." In so many ways we must face the fact that we are like Babylon. We, too, have forgotten our past.

What made America great? What distinguished us from our neighbors to the north and south? Canada was settled by French explorers who were looking for gold. Mexico was settled by Spanish explorers who were also looking for gold. America was settled by men and women who were looking for God. The charters of our original 13 colonies remind us of this. The Rhode Island charter of 1683 says, "We submit our persons, our lives, and our estates to the Lordship of our Lord Jesus Christ, the King of kings and Lord of lords and to all those most perfect and most absolute laws given to us in His Holy Word." Maryland's charter reminds its citizens that it was "formed by a pious zeal to extend the Christian Gospel." Delaware's charter states that it was "formed for the further propagation of the Gospel of the Lord Jesus Christ." And Connecticut was established, in the words of its charter, "to preserve the purity of the Gospel of the Lord Jesus Christ." How have we come so far to now allow our court system to rule against something as simple as placing the Ten Commandments in a courtroom or on a school wall? There's a striking parallel between Babylon and America. Have we lost all sense of remembrance?

Secondly, like Babylon, we seem to have lost a sense of reality. Outside the city of Babylon the Medes and Persians were camped out, but inside Belshazzar and his followers thought they were invincible. They did not face reality. The Lord gave the Israelites who were taken into Babylonian captivity three very important things. He gave them a Lord, a law and a land. Three thousand years later another nation was born. And God did the same thing. He gave America a Lord. Forever etched in the charters of those 13 original colonies is this concrete fact. It is written in stone at places like Harvard. God also gave us a law. The law we have is built and based on Israel's ancient commandments. It, too, is forever etched in the Supreme Court building in Washington, D.C. Also, God gave us a land. And for over 200 years He has protected it. Until September 11, 2001, it had never known attack from an outside invader. Could the fact that we have lost a sense of remembrance and a sense of reality mean that we are following the same path of ancient Babylon? Is God weighing our hearts and is the handwriting on the wall?

It is obvious that we have also lost a sense of restraint. The correlation between moral decay and national decline is written throughout the pages of history with one nation after another. Carl Wilson in his book, *Our Dance Has Turned to Death,* chronicles the pattern of decline in both the Greek and Roman cultures. He says men ceased to lead their families in spiritual and moral development. They neglected their wives and children in pursuit of material wealth and power. Men became so preoccupied with business ventures they ignored their wives' intimate needs and began to be involved with other women. Marriage laws were changed to make divorce easier. Because male and female role models were not in the home, children developed identity problems. Many children were unwanted, aborted, abandoned, molested, left undisciplined. Does this sound a bit familiar to a culture about which we are much more familiar? And this speaks of the demise of a culture of almost 2,000 years ago. Things do not change that much, history simply repeats itself. Yes, the handwriting is on the wall. We seem to have lost our sense of remembrance, reality, and restraint.

Have we also lost a sense of respect? Nothing was sacred to the Babylonians anymore. Because they lived with virtually no moral absolutes it naturally followed that there would be no restraint and thus no respect for anything that was sacred. In Daniel 5 we find Belshazzar drinking his wine from the holy vessels of the temple. We, too, live in a culture that has lost its respect for the things of God. Where are the Daniels of our day saying to our world — *mene, tekel, upharsin?*

The handwriting is on the wall. God is weighing our hearts and speaking to us not only at the point of our pride, not only at the point of our presumption, but especially at the point of our promiscuity.

Chapter 15

God is speaking to us at the point of our perversion

Dan. 5:2-4

Look at the final result of this corrupted Babylonian culture. When one lives by pride and presumption and is governed by promiscuity, one begins to lack any sense of restraint. Nothing was sacred to the Babylonians anymore. Because they had no absolutes it naturally followed that they had no restraints. It was party time in Babylon. The Bible records that Belshazzar was drinking his wine. The verb indicates that he was getting drunk. He was continuing to have one drink after another after another.

There were no restraints. Once he got going he called for the holy vessels that had been brought decades earlier from the temple in Jerusalem. God had said in the Old Testament that they were "holy" unto Him. They were set apart for Himself. These vessels were set apart for God's own special use and purpose in temple worship. In our own culture today some of us might be surprised to see this unfold. However, there are other things that God called holy. That is, separated or set apart for Himself. He called the tithe "holy." He said that one-tenth of our income did not belong to us but was to be set apart for Himself. He called your body "holy." Your body is the temple of the Holy Spirit and is sacred and set apart for His own use. Like the Babylonians, our contemporary culture has few restraints to anything God calls holy.

So into the midst of the banquet hall after the writing on the wall and the hush of the crowd walks our man Daniel. He was not at the party but he was called into it. No one wants the man of God around when liquor is flowing, when the party is in full swing. However, when the handwriting is on the wall, when the crisis time comes, when all our worldly friends have failed, we want to bring in the preacher! Sooner or later the finger of God writes upon the wall and at that moment men and women don't want their immoral friends or drinking buddies. They want someone that can tell them what it means, what God is saying.

Daniel was fully aware of what was transpiring. He knew. He knew how Isaiah, the prophet, scores of years earlier had foretold these events. He knew the Medeo-Persian army was about to enter the city. After all, the handwriting was on the wall! Daniel looked around the scene. The shouting and partying and drinking and open sex had stopped. An eerie silence filled the hall. People seemed to be frozen in time. The sacred vessels were scattered on the floor and on the tables. Spilled wine dripped to the floor. I can imagine the man of God bending over and gently picking up one of the gold goblets from the temple and gracefully, reverently setting it on a table. His heart grieved. But he knew.

Daniel was the only one in the ballroom who was calm. He did what every preacher should do. He took the Word that came from God and without fear or favor just revealed to them all what God had said. This is the preacher's responsibility. Daniel did not coat it over like so many in our contemporary culture do today. He took the Word from the finger of God and simply laid it out.

Look at Daniel. Before he interpreted the handwriting on the wall he preached a sermon to them that had three points. The first point was about power (Dan. 5:18-19). Daniel reminded Belshazzar that King Nebuchadnezzar's power came from God. Yes, *the Most High God gave Nebuchadnezzar your father a kingdom and majesty, glory and honor.* (Dan. 5:18) Belshazzar knew this but had forgotten. Next, Daniel spoke to them about pride. He went on to say, *But when his heart was lifted up and his spirit was hardened in pride, he was deposed from his kingly throne, and they took his glory from him.* (Dan. 5:20) Daniel reminded Belshazzar that King Nebuchadnezzar lost his kingdom because of one word: pride! His final point was about punishment. He reminded his hearers that Nebuchadnezzar *was driven from the sons of men, his heart was made like the beasts, and his dwelling was with the wild donkeys.*

(Dan. 5:21) King Nebuchadnezzar was punished until he realized that the *Most High rules over the affairs of men.* (Dan. 4:32)

After preaching these three points Daniel then began to apply his text. In essence he was saying to Belshazzar, "I've said all this to say to you King Belshazzar, *You have not humbled your heart, although you knew all this.* (Dan. 5:22) Daniel looks into Belshazzar's eyes and reminds him that he knew about the power, the pride, the punishment. On the cross Jesus prayed for forgiveness for those who knew not what they did. But Belshazzar knew. And so do you and I in the midst of our current contemporary culture today. To me the irony of the whole episode is that some of us know better and yet we party on in our own culture when the handwriting is on the wall.

As the partygoers and revelers listened to Daniel's sermon, the hall was hushed. Daniel now reveals God's Word to them. *Mene, tekel, upharsin.* He digs into the lexical roots of these words in order to reveal the three elements involved in the sinners' doom. Their days are numbered. They have been weighed in the balance and found wanting. They will be separated forever. Thus Daniel predicted the end of opportunity. Judgment had come.

Daniel now interpreted each of these words. First, *mene*. This Aramaic noun is derived from the verb meaning "to number". The time has run out. Finished. Over. No more opportunities. No more second chances. Your number is up. You're finished! And that's the way it happens. Suddenly. The finger of God writes on our wall the word *mene* when we least expect it, when we seem to be at rest and flourishing and partying through life. And then, it's over. Finished. This is one of God's truths that we no longer hear from most pulpits in our contemporary American culture anymore. The Bible says *...it is appointed for men to die once, but after this the judgment...*(Heb. 9:27) The Bible challenges us *...to number our days that we may gain a heart of wisdom.* (Ps. 90:12) We just have so many days. They are numbered. Every day we live apart from Christ and His plan for our life we're giving up days that can never be reclaimed. One day our own number will be up. We may be old, we may be middle-aged or we may be young. The handwriting is on the wall. There's coming a day when God will write on our wall *mene*. Therefore, the Psalmist challenges us to *number our days*.

Next is the word *tekel*. The noun is from a verb meaning "to weigh." Daniel presented the picture that they were weighed on a scale. God's standard was on one side, our standard is on the other side. But we are too light. We do not measure up. God's righteous standard is the law. Who could measure up to the righteous demands of the law of God? Who of us has not been weighed and found wanting? Who of us has never broken a law? What a dilemma. What shall we do? More appropriately, what did God do? He sent the Lord Jesus Christ to take our place on the scales of life. He kept the law. He met the righteous standard. He balanced the scales. He never sinned. He was not found wanting in anything. He went to Calvary and took our sin in His own body. He was found wanting for us that we might be free from the righteous demands of the law and be able to step on the scales of life and find favor.

This is why when the word *mene* is written on the wall of our own life, our only hope is to be found in Christ. So that when *tekel* is written we might stand in his righteousness alone which brings the scales into balance. Is it any wonder we used to sing, "My hope is built on nothing less than Jesus' blood and righteousness?"

If you never receive Christ as your personal Savior you'll be weighed on the scales of God by your own life and your own merits. And, when placed alongside the righteous demands of the Word of God, like King Belshazzar, you, too, will be weighed and found wanting. When so many in our culture today are placed on God's scales they will be weighted down by lies and self-seeking, harsh words, unforgiveness, sexual sins, etc. All this fills the scales and it comes crashing down. *Tekel!* Weighed and found wanting. God weighs our motives. God weighs our opportunities. His scales are perfect.

Then came the final word written on the wall of Belshazzar's banquet hall. *Upharsin*. Here's a noun from a verb meaning "to break in two," to separate, to divide. This concept appeared so often during the lifetime of Christ. He divided the sheep from the goats, the wheat from the tares.

Now note the scene in Belshazzar's ballroom. In the midst of this scene of horror and terror was one figure that stood in perfect peace. There was no fright in his face. There was no terror in his eyes. There was no knock in his knees. There was no guilt in his heart. He knew the One who wrote upon the wall. The day of judgment holds no fear for those like Daniel who know the living God.

Daniel Chapter 5 concludes with these words: *That very night Belshazzar, king of the Chaldeans was slain. And Darius the Mede received the kingdom, being about 62 years old.* (Dan. 5:30-31) That very night! While Babylon partied, the armies of the Medes and the Persians diverted the Euphrates into a swampland. The Persian army marched into the walled city through the dry riverbed that ran under the city walls and took the city. God's judgment is sure. There's not a wall high enough nor thick enough to prevent a man nor a nation from falling when God writes on the wall the words *mene, tekel, upharsin.*

Who of us knows how close our own culture is to that word —*mene*. Who of us knows how close we may be to the finger of God writing on our wall *tekel*? Or worse yet, *upharsin.*

What are we personally doing about God and graffiti? Our days are numbered. We are going to be placed on the scales of God and weighed. If we do not measure up we, like so many before us, will be separated.

There is a last night for every nation, and every individual. The handwriting is on the wall. On one side of the scale is God's standard, the righteous demands of His law. Who of us can balance that out? Who of us is not found wanting? What shall we do? That's not the question. What has God already done? He sent the Lord Jesus Christ to take your place on the scales. Jesus came, kept the law, swept our sins off the scales and put in their place His own righteousness. So many in our culture are desperately waiting to hear this good news. They continue to try to stand in their own righteousness and are weighed and found wanting.

Daniel says to Belshazzar, *…it is God who holds your breath in His hand and owns all your ways…* (Dan. 5:23).Think about that. Take a breath. Every breath is a gift of God. He holds your breath in His hand. *Mene, tekel, upharsin.*

As we see the fall of Babylon we cannot help but see some frightening parallels to our own culture. So many of us think we're impregnable, indestructible. We think we could never lose a war or a cause. But the tragedy is we may very well be losing on the inside. Why did Babylon fall? Pride. They were feasting when they should have been fasting. Presumption. They thought they were invincible. Promiscuity. While they were filled with wild, illicit, and unrestrained sex, the end of their world was only hours away. Perversion. They blasphemed God and perverted worship by mocking God and rejecting truth. We are living in a pluralistic culture that tells us there are many ways to God today. In light of eternity what is the kingdom of Babylon or the kingdom of the United States of America when compared with the kingdom forfeited by men and women without Christ, men and women who will be weighed in the balance and found wanting? *Mene, tekel, upharsin.* God and graffiti. The handwriting is on the wall!

Part Six

Integrity —
Don't leave home without it

What is the single most important trait of one who desires to truly make a difference in our culture and world today? Some might say intellect. After all, knowledge is power and many believe that the most important thing they can have in addressing the culture is intellect. Someone else might say intensity, a spirit of conquest, a passion that is contagious. Still others might say it is insight. That is, good old common sense and the ability to see through issues and use discernment. However, in the long run there's one word which describes the single-most important characteristic of one who finishes strongly and makes a lasting difference in the midst of a culture. The word is "integrity." Now, more than ever, it is what our world needs. I've known those with intellect who had keen knowledge and persuasive abilities but who had little or no integrity and are no longer in the race. I've also known those with a tremendous amount of intensity and passion but who had little or no integrity, and they, too, have already dropped by the wayside. I've also known those with a keen insight and the ability to make wise decisions but who ultimately showed that they had little or no integrity and they, too, are out of the race.

Daniel certainly had intellect. We read that he was *...gifted in all wisdom, possessing knowledge and quick to understand...* (Dan. 1:4) He certainly had intensity. The Bible records that Daniel *...purposed in his heart that he would not defile himself...* (Dan. 1:8) He also had insight. We discover this in Daniel Chapter 2 and Chapter 5 when he keenly discerned King Nebuchadnezzar's dream and the handwriting on Belshazzar's wall. However, what truly set Daniel apart from the others and enabled him to achieve such incredible success in Babylon was his integrity. The Bible says, *then this Daniel distinguished himself above the governors and satraps because an excellent spirit was in him...* (Dan. 6:3)

Integrity can be defined as the steadfast adherence to a moral or ethical code. It is the state or quality of being complete; the freedom from corrupting influence or motive. The thesaurus identifies it with such words as honesty, completeness, incorruptibility. In the New King James version of the Bible the word "integrity" appears once in the New Testament. It translates a compound Greek word that contains a negative prefix, the preposition *through*, and the noun *corruption*. The word means that there is no corruption through the man. It speaks of consistency. That is, the word "integrity" defines someone who is in public what he also is in private. Integrity is what causes the professional golfer to turn himself in on an infraction when no one else sees it. It is what causes a witness to tell the truth on the witness stand when no one else will know. Integrity is what keeps employees from cheating on overtime hours or expense accounts. Integrity is what keeps us honest as April 15th rolls around each year. Integrity is what keeps us faithful to our wives or husbands when away on business trips.

Our contemporary culture is crying out to see men and women of integrity. Many of our recent national leaders have sent the wrong messages. We have seen a generation of leaders pass from one moral crisis to another — from Watergate to Monicagate. Scandals have been a part of the highest office of the land. Does anyone see that our culture is reaping the results of the lack of integrity in high places of leadership? It is no wonder polls and voters seem to indicate that character does not count in America anymore. Integrity does not seem to be as important as it used to be.

Our culture seems to be permeated with a void of integrity. Too many cities in America, like my own, have seen widespread investigations in their school districts and city governments. More than one person in Dallas has resigned in disgrace before they were indicted for corruption. Some religious leaders in our cities are no better in this area of integrity. More and more high profile pastors succumb to moral failure and make front page news almost every week. This lack of integrity is rampant in our culture and our world is crying out to see true integrity in the lives of our leaders.

What does all of this have to do with the familiar story of Daniel and the lions' den found in the sixth chapter of Daniel? Most who approach this chapter put their entire focus on Daniel's deliverance from the lions' den. After all, it's one of the most familiar stories in all the Bible. It is among one of the first Bible stories our children learn. Pictures of Daniel lying down with docile lions adorn the walls of our nurseries. However, the real message of Chapter 6 is often overlooked in the familiarity of the lions' den. The real message of this chapter has to do with Daniel's conduct, not while in the lions' den, but before he ever got there! It is a message about integrity and how this character trait was honored by God himself.

Throughout this volume we have watched Daniel time and again engage, influence, and impact the culture around him. In Chapter 1 when he could have lived with resentment and hung his harp on the willow trees, he rested in the fact that God was in control. He reminded us that the Most High rules over the affairs of men. In Chapter 2 he trusted God for all of his tomorrows. In Chapter 3 his three young friends taught us that we have what we tolerate in our own culture. Daniel influenced his culture because he was a man of integrity. He was consistent.

Each of us, like Daniel, lives in the midst of four distinct spheres of life and influence. You have a private life. There's a part of you and me where no one else really goes. Those closest to us, our husbands or wives, do not know all of our private thoughts. No one lives in our own private world except ourselves and God, who truly knows us and searches our heart.

You also have a personal life. This describes that part of you that is shared by a small circle of family and a very few friends who really know you in intimacy. Usually outside of our immediate family it includes only two or three other people who know us as we really and truly are.

We not only have a private life and a personal life, we also have a professional life. This is the part of our world that is a wider circle and consists of dozens or scores of men and women with whom we come into contact weekly at the office or at school or at work or in the civic or social arena.

Finally, we have a public life. This is our widest sphere of influence where anyone and everyone with whom we have dealings is touched with some impression of us throughout the course of the week. Even those we do not know professionally, much less personally or privately, hear our names and form an opinion about us one way or another in the public world. Some people call it our public persona.

Some wonder why there is such little integrity today. Some of us try to put on a good impression publicly where only our public persona or image is projected from a distance. However, when it comes down to the professional level, it's a little harder to disguise. Then, when we enter the level of our personal world it becomes difficult to keep up the act in front of those who really know us in all areas of our lives. Perhaps it is at this point that some preachers' kids fall away as they watch a bit of an image in the public and professional arena they know is a facade because they see something quite different in the personal world. Finally, we come to the private circle. It is here where we only exist with God Himself and we cannot hide from Him.

This brings us to an important question. Where is our integrity rooted? Some think it is rooted in the public life, but it is not, it is only revealed there. Ultimately, it will be revealed whether we have it or not. Others think it is rooted in the professional world where on the anvil of personal experience we beat out the principles of integrity. However, it is not rooted there, it is only reinforced there if we truly have it. Others would be quick to say it is rooted in our personal life where we live in close intimate relationships with one another. But it is not rooted there, it is only reflected there. Integrity is rooted in the private life, that part of us that is alone with God and that part of us that will live as long as God lives. Therefore, once rooted in the private world it flows into the personal level. Here our family and close friends can see something in our interpersonal relationships that is good and godly; that issues out of a private life.

From the personal world integrity then widens to the professional world. Out in the workforce it is reinforced in what we do. Finally, in the public world where our reputation is made our integrity is revealed. Integrity is conceived in the private world, born in the personal world, grows in the professional world, and it matures in the public world for God's glory.

As we seek to address and engage our current, contemporary culture around us, Daniel tells us that there is nothing we can do that will go as far in making a difference than living lives of integrity. Integrity is our most vital asset in addressing the culture. Don't leave home without it!

Chapter 16

Integrity is rooted in our private life

Dan. 6:1-3

After the fall of Babylon, Darius the Mede reorganized the kingdom with 120 governors to whom were delegated authority over all local matters. Over these 120 governors were three commissioners who were assigned to administer the affairs of the kingdom. Daniel was elevated to one of these three commissioners and put in charge of the entire kingdom. *The king gave thought to setting him over the whole realm.* (Dan. 6:3) What was it about Daniel that caused him to stand out above all the others? Time and time again we see him rising to the surface. Something was different about him. It was his integrity and it was rooted in his private life. Daniel 6:3 says *...an excellent spirit was in him.* It wasn't because of what was outside of him. It was because of what was within. We call it integrity. An excellent spirit was within him. This is where integrity finds its roots, in our private world.

Daniel excelled because of an inner strength. In our fast-paced world of self-promotion and "who you know," integrity in the private life is becoming a lost characteristic. Daniel was elevated because of what he was on the inside, not who he knew on the outside. It was his integrity, not his intelligence nor intensity nor insight that brought him into his place of responsibility. Yes, integrity comes from within, not without. It is not rooted in the public life, nor the professional life or even the personal life. Integrity finds its roots in our private world, in the secret place where the Christ-life replaces the self-life.

Integrity stems from an inner power, not an outer promotion. The world has seen enough men and women like those out on the plain of Dura who promote themselves outwardly but have no inner strength, no integrity. At this writing the aged Billy Graham is stricken by disease and is presently in the hospital. Dozens of times people have asked him on talk shows and the like, "Why you? Why is it that you have had a world platform and presidents and kings have sought your counsel?" Integrity is the single thing that has separated Billy Graham from so many others. It is not what he is in public that gives him influence. It is what he has been in private for over half a century that issues out into the public persona. There have been others along the way with keener minds and more persuasive speech, but they are no longer in the race today. How did Billy Graham's influence last so long? What made him so influential, so believable? Was it his intellect? Was it his intensity? No, in a word it was his personal integrity that is rooted in his private life. Solomon had it right; *the integrity of the upright guides them…* (Prov. 11:3)

When the Bible says that Daniel had an excellent spirit in him it simply means that the Spirit of God dominated Daniel's life. It is what is inside of you that gives integrity, not what is outside of you. How do you think of yourself? Do you think of yourself as a body who happens to have a spirit-soul being? Or, do you think of yourself as primarily a spirit-soul being who happens to live in a body? Think about it. Integrity is rooted in the private life. If you're primarily body-conscious, then self-exaltation will manifest itself in your relationships in the personal arena and spill over into the professional arena, and finally, where reputation is made, into the public arena. However, if you are spirit-conscious, then integrity will be rooted in the private world and will ultimately be revealed publicly for the glory of God. We are spirit beings who live in a body that is deteriorating and will one day go back to dust. Integrity is rooted in that part of us that is immaterial, that part of us that will live as long as God lives.

There are two primary tests which come our way in life and have much to do with revealing what is truly in our private life. One is the test of adversity and the other is the test of prosperity. Daniel faced both of them in Chapter 6 and passed with flying colors because of the strength of his inner character and life. Integrity that is rooted in the private life of the spiritual realm is what brings character.

Integrity is often used interchangeably with honesty. We have often heard architects, engineers, or builders say, "this building has structural integrity." That is, the public structure rests upon its private unseen foundation that is solid. The Lord Jesus addressed this point at the end of His famous Sermon on the Mount when He spoke about the wise builder who built his home on the foundation of solid rock. He was speaking of the man of integrity. When an inquirer responded as to the meaning of the solid foundation, our Lord replied that this was the man who hears the Word of God and puts it into practice. Integrity clearly is a matter of the heart. It is rooted in our private world.

Daniel made a difference in his world and culture for 70 years. How? Because of his integrity. Because his integrity was rooted in that private place along with God, then it followed that it was reflected in his personal life and thus reinforced in his professional life and ultimately revealed in his public life for God's glory.

Chapter 17

Integrity is reflected in our personal life

Dan. 6:4-5

Since Daniel's integrity was rooted in his private life, we now see the result was that it was reflected in his personal life. Daniel had an inner circle of close and personal friends not the least of whom were Shadrach, Meshach, and Abednego. Time and again his integrity was reflected in relationships with those who knew him best. It was reflected in front of those who saw him in his most personal moments interacting and interrelating with this small group of friends and associates. His personal life was one of purity and transparency. *He was faithful and there was no error or fault found in him.* (Dan. 6:4) This is quite a statement. His integrity was reflected in his personal world. Think about that statement in verse 4 for just a moment. Those who shared Daniel's most personal moments, those who were his closest confidants, those whose sat in meetings with him and went to lunch with him observed him day by day and said, "He was faithful." Daniel's word was his bond and he could be depended upon. He didn't change with shifting winds of public opinion or personal pressure, much less political expediency. His integrity was reflected in his personal dealings.

An interesting thing develops in Daniel Chapter 6. Those who were in competition, those who were self- promoters and protecting their own turf became quite uncomfortable when someone with integrity came upon the scene. There's a sense in which they're always afraid they'll be exposed. Note that in the plot that develops in this particular chapter, this group of devious individuals stake out his house like reporters hiding in the bushes with a hidden video camera. They bugged his room. But Daniel avoided every appearance of evil. His life was beyond reproach. The Bible says, *they could find no charge or fault because he was faithful...* (Dan. 6:4) Daniel's life matched his lips. He was a man of integrity who had rooted that integrity in the private life and now reflected it in his personal dealings.

Those seeking to investigate him and hoping to find something on him with which to sabotage him could find nothing. The world is a poor judge of our Christianity. However, it is a very sufficient judge of our conduct. I wonder if many of our lives have measured up the scrutiny and surveillance that Daniel went through in Chapter 6 by those who were so filled with jealousy and animosity toward him? Do our private lives spill over into our personal lives as his did?

These evildoers now devised a plot to entrap him. They said, *We shall not find any charge against this Daniel unless we find it against him concerning the law of his God.* (Dan. 6:5) Thus, they came to King Darius with a proposal. They were so filled with jealousy toward Daniel and wanted his position that they sought an evil plot. They brought to the king the plan that *...whoever petitions any god or man for thirty days, except you, O king, shall be cast into the den of lions.* (Dan. 6:7) In fact, they reported to the king that *...all the governors of the kingdom... had consulted together to establish this royal statute...* (Dan. 6:7) That was a lie. All had not agreed. In fact, the main one, Daniel, knew nothing about it. In essence, the plan was to make King Darius god for a month. They appealed to the king's own ego and got him to make a law *...according to the law of the Medes and the Persians.* (Dan. 6:8) This simply meant that this law could never be broken. Thus they sought to put man in God's place. This is the sin of our own day. This was Babylon's sin. This was Rome's sin as the Caesar became known as lord.

It is not much different in modern America. Secular humanism which deifies man is deeply ingrained in our culture today. When those evildoers left the palace of King Darius they were convinced of three things. One, King Darius could not and would not break the decree since it was *according to the law of the Medes and the Persians.* Two, Daniel would never defy his faith in the living God. Three, their plan was foolproof. Now all that was left was to put it into effect.

The decree was made. What will Daniel do now? *Now when Daniel knew that the writing was signed he went home. And in his upper room, with his windows opened toward Jerusalem, he knelt down on his knees three times that day and prayed and gave thanks before his God, as was his custom since early days.* (Dan. 6:10) His integrity which was rooted in the private world is now reflected in the personal world. Daniel simply kept his personal schedule. Consistency was his theme. He went about his prayer time *as was his custom since early days.* Daniel did not change one thing about his lifestyle. All he had to do to save his skin was stop praying openly and publicly for one month. He could have even been subtle about it and at least closed the windows. Or, he could have prayed in bed when his lights were off at night. He could have reasoned that God knew his heart. But Daniel was consistent. That is the mark of a man of integrity. What he was in his personal life is what he was in his private life. Those who are inconsistent with convictions will never be known as people of integrity.

Look at Daniel. He *knelt*. When I read the text I personally stopped at this word. I was impressed at how Daniel got down on his knees to pray. So many of us today are too sophisticated or perhaps too proud or maybe even too sensitive about how it looks to others to get down on our knees and pray. I'm so thankful there's a pattern for all of us here.

We can learn much about the secret life of Daniel. (Dan. 6:10) He had a set time when he prayed. He had a set place in which he prayed. He had a set posture when he prayed. And, what kind of prayer did he pray? He prayed a prayer of thanksgiving. Daniel was consistent. He thanked God in days of delight when things were going his way and he thanked God in days of difficulty when they were not. Daniel did not wait until the crisis hour to find his strength. This was *his custom*. This consistent integrity had been the practice of his personal life since his teenage years when he *purposed in his heart not to eat the king's meat*. (Dan. 1:8)

Daniel is showing us that to have influence and to make a difference in our culture, integrity is the key. We might have all the intellect and intensity and insight in the world but without integrity we will never influence our culture. Integrity is rooted in our private world, and consequently, it is then reflected in our personal world.

Chapter 18

Integrity is reinforced in our professional life

Dan. 6:4-10

What about your professional life — that sphere of life that is ever widening? If integrity is, in fact, rooted in the private world, it will be reflected in the personal world and thus reinforced in the professional world. Note that as Daniel's jealous peers sought to find fault with him they sought to find it *concerning the kingdom.* (Dan. 6:4) That is, the government affairs of his professional life. Those who have integrity find that it is reinforced in the professional life. One of the first places integrity truly shows up is in our employment. They could find nothing wrong with Daniel in the discharge of his duties. (Dan. 6:4) Proverbs 20:6-7 says, *Most men will proclaim each his own goodness...the righteous man walks in his integrity.* Integrity is reinforced on the anvil of personal experience in the marketplace. One of the biggest problems with businesses today is in finding personnel. Many business owners do not have to be as concerned with outsiders stealing from them as much as they do insiders. Kickbacks are a common theme in many organizations. Integrity is a lost word in the professional life of many people.

How should we as Christian employees behave? Integrity should be reinforced in our professional lives. Paul makes this very clear in Ephesians Chapter 6. He addresses the point clearly. He says, *…be obedient to those who are your masters… with sincerity of heart as to Christ.* (Eph. 6:5) Men and women of integrity are characterized in the marketplace by obedience. They recognize authority. The one thing the Christian worker is commanded to do is obey those in authority over him. As Christians we're not anarchists. We do not believe in the abolition of authority. We recognize authority in the home, in government, in the church, why shouldn't we recognize it also in the marketplace? They could find no charge or fault in Daniel *…because he was faithful* (Dan. 6:4)

One of the problems in America today is leisure time. Some of us who are quick to *remember the Sabbath* (Ex. 20:8) forget that the Bible also says, *six days you shall labor and do all your work.* (Ex. 20:9) When you show up for work on time, give an honest day's work, are loyal to your employer, you are doing what you ought to do as a Christian. We ought to be extra-loyal, extra-enthusiastic, extra-hardworking. We ought to be the second milers about whom Jesus spoke. This is Christian integrity being reinforced in the professional life. When we sit at our desk and daydream, read the paper or novels, or listen to talk radio while at the office, it is a poor witness for Christ in the marketplace. The best way integrity can be reinforced on the job is to give a full day's work. The Christian realizes that his time is not his own but it belongs to his employer. We have no right to use our employer's time for our own personal endeavors, even to evangelize. What if the cashier at the grocery store stopped and witnessed to everyone who came through the checkout line? There is a sense in which when we take our own time on the job, we steal time from our employer. If you work for someone else and do not give them eight hours in an eight-hour workday you are not reinforcing integrity. If you come in late, loaf around on the job, take extra time for lunch, spend a little bit longer on breaks, you are as much of a thief as if you robbed a bank. If you are paid for eight hours and you slough off an hour and work only seven hours, in essence you have stolen an hour's pay. You might as well have gone to the petty cash drawer and taken it out when no one was looking.

The believer is to be a person of integrity in the faithful discharge of his duties. Like Daniel, there should be found *no charge or fault in us*. Paul also says in Ephesians 6 that we are to serve our employers *not with eyeservice, as men-pleasers, but as bondservants of Christ, doing the will of God from the heart…*(Eph. 6:6) This speaks of those who keep an eye on the boss more than they do on the task. The believer should do the same quality work in the absence of supervision as he does in the presence of it. The marketplace today is our biggest opportunity to engage our culture and transform it by personal integrity. Those with integrity should not be "men-pleasers." Some are obsessed with what he or she thinks about this or that. Some people's entire lives are controlled by the opinions of others. Those with integrity don't poll popular opinions before making decisions. Why? Because their integrity is not only rooted in their private life and reflected in their personal life, it is reinforced in their professional life.

Paul goes on in the Ephesians epistle to conclude that we are to do our work *with goodwill doing service as to the Lord and not to men.* (Eph. 6:7) This was Daniel's philosophy. As followers of Christ we are serving the Lord whether we work in a textile mill, a service station, a high-rise office building, an assembly line, a hospital, or behind a desk in some office. As believers we are on our honor. Integrity is reinforced in the professional life. When we work *as to the Lord* it gives labor a new dignity. When the waitress in the restaurant serves the customer *as to the Lord* it brings dignity to what she does. When the medical doctor attends to each patient *as to the Lord* it brings dignity to what he or she does. Can you imagine what would happen in our culture if believers in the marketplace began to capture the philosophy that Daniel had and Paul wrote about? If our culture is ever to be addressed and transformed, it must take place in the marketplace — not in the church house.

Our greatest opportunity to make a difference and engage our culture is in the same place it was in Babylon — out there in the marketplace. It is imperative that as Christians we be men and women of integrity who reinforce that integrity in our professional life. There is a very small percentage of our cities in church on any given Sunday morning. However, on Monday we scatter into the workforce by the multiplied thousands and touch hundreds of thousands of lives for good or bad. This is how the Christian faith spread in the first century in its most explosive growth. Men and women with integrity became salt and light every day, everywhere they were.

Our culture is much like the culture in exile we find in the book of Daniel. Who made a difference here? The preachers who came into exile? No, the laymen. Men like Daniel, civil servants and politicians, people like Nehemiah, faithful laymen who reinforced their integrity in the professional world. Daniel was a man of integrity. It showed in his professional life. Those with integrity stand out above others in the workplace. This is also true in the school or in the community.

Daniel is our classic example of a man whose integrity was not only rooted in the private world and reflected in the personal world, but reinforced in the professional world. We cannot begin a life of integrity in the professional arena. We must have it before we get there. It is not rooted there but it surely is reinforced there. Integrity is the most important ingredient we can have in engaging our culture. Don't leave home without it.

Chapter 19

Integrity is revealed in our public life

Dan. 6:11-28

Now Daniel is thrust into the spotlight of the public arena for all to see. Daniel's commitment to God was public. It was not simply practiced behind closed doors. His commitment was not something he compartmentalized on Sunday morning and left in the box on Monday through Friday. Here was a man, not a preacher but a civil servant, a business administrator, a politician, if you please, who because his integrity was rooted in the private life is now revealed in the public life. Once we're thrust into the public life it is too late to look for integrity if we don't already have it. Daniel's deliverance from the lions' den was *because he believed in his God.* (Dan. 6:23) What he was in private was revealed in public.

What an evening we read about here in Daniel Chapter 6. Daniel is thrown in the midst of a den of hungry lions. But he slept like a baby that night. King Darius was up all night pacing back and forth, concerned and confused. At dawn he rushed to the lions' den, cupped his hands and shouted, *Daniel, servant of the living God, has your God whom you serve continually, been able to deliver you from the lions?* (Dan. 6:20) Daniel awakens, rubs his eyes, stretches out his arms, wipes the lion's hair from his head where he had pillowed his head, and answers, *O king, live forever. My God sent His angel and shut the lions' mouths, so that they have not hurt me, because I was found innocent before him; and also O king, I have done no wrong before you.* (Dan. 6:21-22) The king's question to Daniel is one our culture is asking us today. "Is our God whom we serve able to deliver us?"

Daniel's faith won the victory. The Bible says he was delivered because *he believed in his God.* (Dan. 6:23) It is one thing to face adversity when we've done wrong. It is another to face it when we've done right. Daniel did not panic, he simply kept his faith in God. This is the mark of true integrity that is rooted in the private world. It follows that it finally is revealed in the public world.

There is a lesson here for all of us. Daniel was not in the lions' den because he had done something wrong. He was there because he had done something right! It seems confusing doesn't it? In our world it is not always true that if we do wrong, we'll be punished and if we do right, we'll be rewarded. Sometimes the opposite seems to be true. Some people like Daniel pay a big price for doing the right thing. Paul listed the heroes of our faith in the eleventh chapter of Hebrews and although Daniel is not mentioned by name there we do read these words in verse 33, *who through faith subdued lions, worked righteousness, obtained promises and stopped the mouths of lions...* Daniel's God is our God! Integrity is revealed in the public arena.

Note the outcome of the experience of the lions' den. Daniel did not take credit for the victory. He was quick to say, *My God sent His angel and shut the lions' mouths...* (Dan. 6:22) A man of integrity does not take credit for something God does. Daniel did not exalt himself but exalted his Lord before the king and the people. Thus King Darius made a decree. *To all peoples, nations, and languages that dwell in all the earth: peace be multiplied to you. I make a decree that in every dominion of my kingdom men must tremble and fear before the God of Daniel. For He is the living God, and steadfast forever; His kingdom is the one which shall not be destroyed, and His dominion shall endure until the end. He delivers and rescues, and He works signs and wonders in heaven and on earth, who has delivered Daniel from the power of the lions. So this Daniel prospered in the reign of Darius and the reign of Cyrus the Persian.* (Dan. 6:25-28) The world stops to take notice of the man of integrity. Integrity is revealed in the public life. Sooner or later this is always true.

What do we learn from Daniel's experience in the lions' den? We learn that integrity is rooted in the private world. Prayer should be a priority. Daniel was willing to die for it.

On the scale of Daniel's value system, his private time alone with God was a high priority. He knew that integrity was rooted in the private world.

We have also learned that integrity is reflected in the personal world. How we respond in our personal relationships with those who know us best is in direct correlation to the strength of our own private life. There was no error found in Daniel because it was his habit to meet his God in the secret place.

We have also learned that true integrity is reinforced in the professional world. Integrity is crucial in the marketplace. Some of us have the idea that our faith belongs in one world and our work belongs in another. Some of us do not truly impact our culture because there is not much difference in our lives on Monday through Friday than the lives of those with whom we work. Our culture will never be addressed and engaged for the cause of Christ unless it's done in the marketplace. Daniel is our example of what it means to keep our integrity in the midst of high pressure and even unfair circumstances.

We also learned that integrity is ultimately revealed in the public life. Everything King Darius knew about God he learned by observing Daniel's public life of integrity. We're being watched and the world is asking *…has your God whom you serve continually, been able to deliver you from the lions?* (Dan. 6:20) And, they will never know unless we are men and women of integrity.

Our current, contemporary culture brings new challenges to our Christian faith with each passing day. Daniel was a young man who grew up like many of us, rooted in a Judeo culture of traditional family values. One day, also like us, he unexpectedly found himself in a culture that was foreign to everything that he had known. His value system, his truth claims, his moral compass was challenged repeatedly at every turn. His world evolved into a world of pluralism and paganism. But Daniel had a different spirit in him. He was a man of integrity who not only addressed his culture but also engaged it and influenced it for good. Daniel's God is our God. The challenge to us is to: "dare to be a Daniel, dare to stand alone, dare to have a purpose firm, and dare to make it known!" Integrity: don't leave home without it!